TIME MANAGEMENT
FOR NETWORK MARKETERS

INCREASING PERSONAL PRODUCTIVITY

Garry A. Ford • Harold L. Taylor • Carol Ford

"If you are interested in taking control of your time, earning more money and getting more out of life... buy and apply this book." ~ Tom Stoyan, Canada Sales Coach

Time Management for Network Marketers
Written by Garry A. Ford, Harold L. Taylor and Carol Ford

Copyright ©2014, Phoenix Consulting & Contract Management Inc.
10661 Chinguacousy Road, Box 70044, Brampton ON L7A 0N5

All rights reserved. No part of this publication may be reproduced, stored in a retrieval system, or transmitted in any form or by any means, electronic, mechanical, photocopying, recording or otherwise without the written permission of Phoenix Consulting & Contract Management Inc.

Edited by Carol Ford
Printed in Canada

BOOK DEDICATION

This book is lovingly dedicated to the late Marlene Patricia Taylor, devoted wife of Harold L. Taylor for over 38 years. Marlene was an inspiration to everyone she met and she supported and encouraged Harold throughout his successful career in time management training and consulting.

Marlene left us in May 2013, after a heroic ten-year battle with cancer. We all miss her, but recall with great fondness the legacy she has left behind.

FOREWORD

Anyone who is building a network marketing business knows that they are working with a unique business model. While most people have a "day" job where they go to work in the morning and go home to their family and relax in the evening, a network marketer has a different schedule. He may go to work all day, but instead of taking the evenings and weekends to relax, he invests this time in his new business. The hopes and the dreams of most network marketers is that their new business will replace their current job so they can be their own boss and earn what they feel they truly deserve – gaining better control of their own time and finances. Tens of thousands of people are living proof that this can happen.

What is required to be a successful network marketer is the ability to manage one's time and to focus on the long-term better than traditional workers do. You must learn and apply new skills of personal organization, planning, scheduling, and managing a team with all the time management and strategies that such a focus entails. At times you may feel like a juggler, trying to keep several balls in the air successfully at the same time. That may be a time when you feel like giving up, but this book is your roadmap to achieving control of your time schedule, placing your focus and energy where it will count, and learning how you conduct yourself while building a successful network marketing business. If that is what you truly desire and are committed to, then this book is designed for you.

One of the authors, Harold Taylor has been in the time management consulting business for almost forty years. He has written 20 books, addressed thousands of audiences, and trained more people in time management techniques than just about any other person in the world. Even today, as the CEO of Harold Taylor Time Consultants, Harold still writes a monthly newsletter, delivers frequent seminars, workshops, webinars, and teleconferences, and is constantly working on additional books.

The other two authors, Garry and Carol Ford, have been in the direct selling industry since 1977. They have respectively managed several companies and consulted to many others. During their careers they have coached thousands of network marketers. Garry has written a book along those lines called "Coaching Your Downline to Become Your Successline". That title should speak for itself. In 2012, Garry received a Queen's Jubilee Medal for his lifetime of service to the direct selling industry. Carol has not only served in senior executive positions in networking marketing, but she has also owned two direct selling companies and has been an independent distributor with a number of companies. This vast experience is now shared in the industry as she coaches network marketers to enjoy the experiences that she and Garry have been blessed with. Garry, serves as President of Harold Taylor Time Consultants Ltd, and coaches network marketers specifically in the area of time management.

It is the authors' hope that if you are one of those fortunate people who has discovered the magic of networking marketing, that this book will save you hours of wasted time and help you to increase your productivity – becoming more organized at developing and leading your dream team.

Remember, you can't manage time. All you can do is manage yourself with respect to time.

We wish you great success!

Garry, Harold and Carol

Table of Contents

Dedication	Page 3
Foreword	Page 4
Table of Contents	Page 5
Introduction	Page 6

Chapter 1: Set goals and priorities — Page 11
The advantages of goal-setting. What do you want from life? Characteristics of goals. You're never too old. Making your goals achievable. Programming your mind for success. Maintaining balance in your life.

Chapter 2: Plan and schedule — Page 21
Budgeting your time. Determining your priorities. The danger of To Do lists. Transforming goals into activities. Using the Taylor planner. Keeping interruptions to a minimum. Stacking activities.

Chapter 3: Write things down — Page 34
Telephone & Visitor's Log. Delegation Record. Telephone Directory. Meeting Participant's Action Sheet. Don't rely on your memory. Away from the business.

Chapter 4: Don't procrastinate — Page 44
What is procrastination? How we procrastinate. Overcoming procrastination. Five-step action plan. Getting an early start. Making a commitment to act.

Chapter 5: Don't be a packrat — Page 56
Packrats lose time, money and space. Getting rid of the backlog. Reducing the paperwork flow. Coping with the information explosion. Handling junk mail. Keeping files thin. Looking for timesavers. Handling incoming mail.

Chapter 6: Store things in an orderly way — Page 69
Organizing your personal office. The use of binders. Controlling your environment. The use of labels. The follow-up file. Keeping a clear desk. Personalizing your filing system. The alpha-numerical file system. Hints for effective filing. Organization in the home.

Chapter 7: Work smarter, not harder — Page 80
Principles of delegation. Ask your upline to delegate. Searching for better ways to do things. Making meetings more effective. Utilizing travel time. Managing the telephone.

Chapter 8: Avoid the tyranny of the urgent — Page 89
Focusing on your goals. Keeping your life in perspective. The hurry & wait society. A little pressure is a good thing. Time hassles. Personality and stress. Learning to recognize stress. Haste makes waste.

Chapter 9: Take charge of technology — Page 101
In a world that places much emphasis on technology, learn to apply only that which enhances efficiency.

Epilogue — Page 107
Putting the ideas into practice. The difference between mechanical ideas and behavioral ideas. Forming habits.

Time Management Checklist — Page 109
50 time-tested ways of improving your personal productivity

Concluding Words	Page 111
Recommended Resources	Page 113
Endorsements	Page 114

INTRODUCTION

The value of time

The three major resources that are necessary in order to operate a successful business are time, money, and people.

If you lose money, you can always earn or borrow more. If you lose people, you can sponsor others. But if you lose time, you can never regain it - either by working or by borrowing. It is lost forever. And the sad part is, there is not an inexhaustible supply. You can dip into the time bank only so many times - then, once it's all gone, you're gone.

It stands to reason that since time is in great demand and it is in such limited supply, that it is the most valuable resource. Therefore, if you want to be successful in business, you must learn to manage the time at your disposal.

Unfortunately, some people can't even manage their money, let alone their time. And even some of those who *do* manage their money well do a relatively *poor* job of managing their time. The expression, "Look after the pennies and the dollars will look after themselves" is equally true for this precious commodity called time. We cannot afford to be spendthrifts when it comes to time. Spending time on impulse items such as dawdling over junk mail, thumbing through magazines, rearranging furniture and repositioning paintings when there are meaningful tasks to be performed is one way we squander valuable minutes, which soon amount to hours.

We also waste time by constantly shuffling papers, searching for misplaced items, interrupting ourselves and others needlessly, procrastinating on jobs that *must* be done eventually, worrying about things we can't control, and saying "yes" to time-consuming activities that do not relate to our goals.

Add to this perfectionism, idle time, and a myriad of bad habits, and we have the potential to waste hours each day. Hours that could be spent on profit-generating activities, family time, or self-renewal.

Get organized

The first step in gaining control of your time is to get organized. Organize your office, your files and your procedures to eliminate those wasted minutes searching for things, shuffling papers and interrupting others. Then look for shortcuts when performing those necessary but routine activities such as corresponding, conducting meetings, and fielding phone calls. The resulting time savings can then be invested in those profit- generating activities and personal priorities that you just haven't had time for.

Time management is not a one-time thing. It is a continuous process of changing time wasting habits, streamlining the necessary activities, and focusing always on those key activities that generate the greatest return.

Time management could be viewed as common sense or self-management. It may seem easy. But it isn't easy for one reason; we are forced to change ways that we are comfortable with - habits that we have developed over the years. Change does not come easily. It takes motivation, determination, and perseverance. But the rewards, a more productive and satisfying life, are worth the effort.

Where do we start?

We start by recognizing those habits that cause time problems for ourselves and others. People who have watched our *Making Time Work for You* DVD (www.taylorintime.com) have recognized themselves in some of the situations being role-played by Harold. They then had to muster up enough motivation to actually make some changes to their own work habits.

Some people shrug off their disorganization by claiming they were born that way. Others claim they are so organized they were born on their due dates. But personal organization is not hereditary. You acquire your habits, good or bad, as you grow older. The more bad habits you have acquired, the more difficult it is to get organized; but it *can* be done.

That's the good news. The bad news is it takes effort. Nothing worthwhile comes easily. Anyone can resolve to get up a half hour earlier, for example; but actually getting up requires effort. It takes varying degrees of effort to put things back after using them, purge the files, develop the "do it now" habit, and tear yourself away from pleasant but unproductive tasks.

So you must want to get organized badly enough to endure some temporary unpleasantness. You must be self-motivated. No seminar, book, or DVD is ever going to give you the incentive to persist in your efforts to get organized. That's a fact that you must accept.

How do we become self-motivated?

So where does the motivation come from? Motivation(M) is a product of the amount of desire (AD) to get organized multiplied by the expectancy that you will succeed(AS) .It reads like this: ADxAS=M. So if you are experiencing few problems the way you are, and are happy with the results you are achieving, you will have a low desire to change. But if you are convinced that you can get more accomplished and lead a better life if you were more time-effective, your desire will be high. It only remains for you to be convinced that certain changes *will* lead to personal organization.

And confirmation of that is available from individuals who have succeeded in changing habits and increasing their effectiveness. So read the books on goal-setting, success and time management authored by individuals who *did* succeed using their own methods. There are plenty of testimonials that goal-setting, planning, self-discipline and persistence pay off. If you believe it, and you want it b a d l y e n o u g h for yourself, you will *have* the motivation.

Make changes gradually

A word of caution: don't try to change too many things at once. Remember, time management is a life-long process. Make change gradually. Become comfortable with using a Telephone Log for example, before revamping the way you conduct yourself in other areas.

Where do you get your ideas? There are over 800 books on the topic of time management. (At least that's how many are in our library at this time.) Articles appear almost every month in one of the thousands of magazines and newsletters being published. There is no shortage of ideas on saving time. But what you must do is select those ideas you feel will work for you. Adapt them, if necessary, to suit your particular situation, then put them into practice.

Summary

Time does not pass. We do. Don't try to control time or you will simply become frustrated. Time cannot be managed, saved, stored, stopped, or spent. So stop concentrating on *time* and focus your attention on something you *can* influence - *yourself.* Use time only as a measuring stick to determine how effective you can become. Can you increase the number of significant accomplishments within the same time frame? Or can you achieve what you are now achieving in a shorter period of time? Once you start concentrating on something you *can* control, yourself, you w i l l eliminate many of the frustrations experienced when you try to control others, or time itself - over which you have little or no control. And strange as it may seem, when you start managing *yourself,* many of the problems you were blaming on the clock - or others - disappear.

Ask yourself some basic questions:

Do I have a clear set of personal goals in writing?

Saving time is to no avail if you have nothing meaningful to spend it on. Examine yourself and your values. Determine what is important to you and what you would like to accomplish in your lifetime. Then, put these aspirations into the form of specific objectives that you can work towards.

Do I use my planner properly?

Use it to record more than people appointments and meetings; use it to plan your week in advance. Jot down specific days and times when you plan to work on that project, report, article, sales call or counseling session. Fill your planner with priorities that relate to your goals so there's no room for the trivia.

Am I writing things down instead of relying on my memory?

Many ideas and opportunities are lost, mistakes made, and communications stifled simply because we relied on our memories. Always carry a notepad with you or record essential information on your cell phone. Record telephone calls, actions resulting from meetings, ideas that pop into your head, assignments given and received, deadline dates and dates of events such as birthdays, conferences, and reviews.

Am I procrastinating?

Many people have goals that are really only intentions. Because they never get around to working on them. They are sidetracked by those urgent but unimportant activities that seemingly must be done. Or they gravitate towards those pleasant or easy tasks that consume their time. Reducing procrastination is essential if you are to lead a fruitful life and achieve a sense of accomplishment.

Am I a packrat?

Are you among the many people in this country who are drowning in their possessions? Do you have drawers, files, and cabinets filled with things you never use? Paperwork alone has become a real problem for many people. It is difficult to be organized when there is simply too much to organize.

Do I work in a disorganized environment?

People waste valuable time searching for things, shuffling papers, interrupting themselves, and jumping from one job to another simply because their work area is disorganized. Spend a day - or evening - cleaning out your desk drawers, eliminating unnecessary paperwork, developing a simple file system, follow-up file and project files. Decide where you will store each item and stick to it. Stop using the desk top as a storage area, clear out your in-basket daily, and take the few seconds necessary to put away a project once you have finished working on it for the time being. You will work better if you are organized.

Am I working smarter rather than harder?

Are you using up valuable time on jobs that can be delegated, assigned, or contracted out to others? You have a limited amount of time; it never varies. So make sure you fill it with those priority activities that only you can perform. For example, don't spend three hours of your life washing your car when you can have it done for you for six dollars. (Unless, of course, your time is not worth two dollars per hour, or there's nothing else you'd rather do than wash cars.) Always search out better ways of doing things.

Am I caught up in the tyranny of the urgent?

If you keep yourself busy enough you won't notice that you're not accomplishing anything. Are you constantly under time pressures, fighting to keep your head above water? You must divorce yourself from the rat race, modify your sense of time urgency, and concentrate on the 20% of the activities that produce 80% of the results.

If you have asked yourself these eight questions, and are not satisfied with the answers, read the following chapters. Each of these eight areas will be discussed in detail. Pick those ideas that will work best for you, and put them into practice.

CHAPTER 1

SET GOALS AND PRIORITIES

Most people think they are goal-oriented, but they are really only wish-oriented. People want to travel, write, speak, run their own business, live in the country, learn to fly, earn a college degree ad infinitum. But are these things goals or simply desires? How much time are they really prepared to devote each week to these pursuits? A goal-oriented person does more than just *wish* for something. He or she actually puts it in writing, establishes a deadline, schedules time each day (or each week), and *spends* that time engaged in an activity that will help achieve that goal.

Having a desire for something is one thing. Having a specific, measurable goal in writing, with a plan of action to achieve it is something else. A dream is okay; but there is little chance of achieving a dream. Reduce it to writing, and if it is definite, measurable, realistic, and you are willing to match your desire with an equal measure of commitment, it becomes a goal. If you want to be successful you must become goal-oriented, not wish-oriented.

The advantages of goals

Mark Lee, in his book, *How to Set Goals and Really Reach Them*, claims that to have a goal in mind and work for its accomplishment is an exciting adventure that will increase your sense of well-being. "It tones the body, mind and spirit. Goal-oriented persons seem healthier, happier and more confident than non goal-oriented persons. They appear to be at the controls, to be leaders, and to be problem solvers. Non goal-oriented persons seem to be troubled, rather than animated, with problems. They are more likely to blame *others* for failure or omission for which *they* should take responsibility." He also makes the point that goals provide a means to the human sense of accomplishment.

Goals are a necessary ingredient of time management, since it is goals that allow us to differentiate between the real priorities and the other activities that tend to sidetrack us.

Personal goal-setting is a pre-requisite for personal growth, self-improvement and success. Goals add purpose and lend direction to life. Without goals, we drift. It is essential to have goals at all stages of our lives - for school, career *and* retirement. The trouble with the philosophy, "eat, drink and be merry, for tomorrow we may die" is that we may not. Life expectancy has come a long way - from about 40 years in 1850 to over 75 years at the present time. And goals may very well help *extend* our lifespan even beyond those statistics.

In summary, goals...
- Create a climate for motivation
- Enable us to plan and gain greater control over our own destinies
- Add challenge to our lives and a sense of achievement
- Provide a means of self-evaluation
- Make us results-oriented so we work smarter, not harder
- Add a new dimension of meaning to our lives
- Enable us to manage our time more effectively
- Reduce the stress normally attributed to the feeling of "not getting anywhere"
- Increase our chances of success
- Allow us to determine whether our activities and business are compatible with the things we really want out of life

What do you want from life?

In spite of the advantages of goal-setting and the personal endorsements given to it by successful goal-setters, it is not widespread. According to Paul Zimmerman, president of a financial planning firm, among high income persons,

- more than half have no wills
- many have little idea of family worth
- most have inadequate tax counsel
- less than half plan financially for their children's education
- many don't know their own company benefits

Few successful people will deny that there is a direct relationship between their goal-setting and their success. And since an estimated 95% of the population have no clear-cut goals in writing, it isn't difficult to get ahead of the pack.

Goal-setting is a powerful tool. There is no limit to what you can achieve, given the time and motivation to do so. Within ten years you can effect a complete career change, obtain a PhD in Psychology, save enough money to tour Europe, launch a successful business, rise to executive level in a large corporation - or even become a billionaire or best-selling author or well-known radio and TV personality.

But to achieve any of these things you must (a) honestly ask yourself if you really *want* to, and (b) establish a *written* goal to that effect, along with short-term objectives that progressively lead to that goal. If you're not sure what you want out of life and what it is you want to do or accomplish, start thinking about it right now.

To get started on this self-analysis, jot down any of the following items that appeal to you. Add others that come to mind. Some of the items you jot down or add may become the basis of a goal in itself. Others will keep you from setting a goal that would be in conflict with those things you really enjoy in life. Here are a few examples to get you thinking:

- Running your own business
- Having an interesting career
- Having a happy, satisfying marriage
- Spending time with interesting friends
- Having a comfortable home in the suburbs, or city or country
- Living in a modern apartment resort in the heart of an exciting city
- Producing a great work of art or best-selling novel
- Having enough free time and money to travel
- Getting to really know and understand your family, spending quality time with them
- Staying in good physical condition
- Having people consult with you because you are an expert in one particular field
- Making enough money to travel
- Educating your children in a prestige institution
- Buying whatever luxuries you desire
- Working in a high-level job and influencing the direction of a major corporation
- Having an interesting hobby
- Spending time in meditation, prayer, and spiritual development
- Retiring at the age of 55, 65 or 70
- Changing careers or going back to school

Can you think of any others? Conduct a brainstorming session with yourself, or better still, with your family. Write down what you really enjoy doing. What gives you a sense of satisfaction, achievement, self-esteem, personal growth? Then, from the list, select a few priorities - those things you want above everything else - and see if you can express them in terms of goals. For example, if authoring a best-selling novel appeals to you and you think you will feel the same way in the future, one of your goals might be "to complete a 100,000 word novel by a specific date that has the *potential* to become a best-seller." (No author can actually write a best-seller; the publisher, media, and the public determine its success.)

Your shorter term objectives might include things like "complete a 10-week fiction writing course at Ryerson University by June 15th", "qualify for your company's next incentive trip by November 15th" and so on. Your goals and objectives should be well thought out and reduced to writing. They must be realistic, measurable, and compatible with one another and with your desired lifestyle. You must have the self-discipline to pursue each short-term goal relentlessly, focusing on the rewards of the eventual achievement and not on the temporary discomfort of the pursuit.

A seminar trainer once suggested that if you keep participants busy enough, they won't realize they're not learning anything. The same thing applies to life; if you keep yourself busy enough, rushing from job to job, you won't realize you're not *getting* anywhere.

It's important to stop from time to time and take inventory. One thing's certain. If you find you *do* want to achieve something, chances are you *can* do it . . . if your desire to succeed is strong enough. It has often been pointed out that we tend to become precisely what we imagine ourselves to be. All that we need are concrete goals and a step-by-step plan of action.

So, don't *wait* for opportunities, make your own. If you want to get something in the *future,* the time to start is *now,* in the *present.* Don't be afraid to put your ambitions in writing. And don't be discouraged by the fact that your goals may not be reached for another five or more years. It's better to aim for success in the long run than never know what success feels like.

If you have not drawn up goals for your personal and professional life, try it. If you feel you don't *need* goals to succeed, try this: Think ahead ten years. Where will you be if you make no changes to your present career, lifestyle, education, investment portfolio, etc.? How old will you and your family be? What education will the children be able to afford? What job will you be working at? How much money will you be earning? What will you own? What hobbies will you have? What high points will you be able to look back on? If you're happy with what you see, you probably *don't* need goals. That's where you'll be. But don't kid yourself, if you're not saving money now, or not spending time with the family now, or not attending university now, what makes you think anything will be different in the future? We all tend to procrastinate, and if you have not made an effort to start on those things now, it's unlikely you'll be doing those things in the future. Unless you set goals now, and set those goals in motion.

If you're not happy with what you see when you extrapolate what you are doing now to ten years from now, repeat the process. But this time assume that your dreams have come true. What does this new scenario look like? You may see yourself as a more successful, happier individual with greater skills, accomplishments, interests and achievements. If you prefer this to the first scenario, draw up specific goals for yourself, and formulate a plan to reach those goals.

Characteristics of goals

To increase your chances of achieving the goals you decide upon, follow the following guidelines.

- Put your goals in writing. Otherwise, they're just dreams or wishes. If they're realistic, they can always be expressed in words. Writing them down makes you focus on them and provide commitment.

- Make sure they're realistic. Check them like this: can they be reached by anyone with the same abilities and opportunities as you? If so, they're realistic.

- Avoid pie-in-the-sky goals which are beyond your reach.

- Be specific. You have to be able to measure them so don't write down vague goals such as "to be happy", "to be fulfilled", "to be rich" or "to be intellectually mature". Think of the things that would make you happy or fulfilled and put them down in concrete terms. For example, a measurable goal would be to earn $150,000 per year as a network marketer by May 31st in a specific year.

- List your goals in order of priority. You may not be able to accomplish them all. Which ones are most important to you? Work on these first.

- Make sure that your goals are compatible with one another and that they are compatible with goals of your spouse or family members, too. One of your goals could involve starting up your own business while you are still employed full time. Another goal could be to spend more quality time with your family. The two may not be compatible. Which one is more important to you? Can one of them be changed? Can one be temporarily sacrificed? Can you achieve both by selecting a certain type of business? Remember that it's personal goals that provide meaning and direction to your life. That's one of the beauties of owning a network marketing business.

Understand that it makes sense to be proactive through planning – to visualize possible consequences before they occur and act before they can happen. Through the process of goal setting and planning you can influence the future. For further information on the goal setting process, you might refer to our book, *Say Yes to Your Dreams. (available at www.taylorintime.com as an ebook)*

Goals can keep you young

Regardless of your age, whether you're nine or ninety, goal-setting will work for you. Never use the excuse that you're too old. LeRoy (Satchell) Page, who played professional baseball in his 60's, once asked the question, "How old would you be if you didn't know how old you were?" Which is another way of saying that you are only as old as you feel. Unfortunately, in our society we tend to pigeonhole people at arbitrarily selected ages. We're an adult at 21, middle-aged at 50, old at 70 and ancient at 80. Some seniors actually believe what they hear and start acting and talking accordingly. "I'm too old for sports", "You can't teach an old dog new tricks", "My memory's going", are common remarks made by people in their sixties and seventies. They hear that they're supposed to be old, they think it, the self-fulfilling prophecy takes over, and soon they *are* old. At least, mentally. But we don't suddenly become old. Life is a gradual aging process that starts the day we're born. And living one day at a time until we die will prevent us from categorizing ourselves as middle-aged or old.

One study of high achievers revealed that 64 percent of their accomplishments were attained after age 60. So we're certainly not *over the hill* as far as our careers are concerned. Here are a few examples of people who were successful in their senior years: Ronald Reagan was president of the United States while in his seventies. Winston Churchill became Prime Minister of Great Britain at age 65. Oliver Wendell Homes, Jr. became U.S. Supreme Court Justice at age 61 and served until he was 92. Pablo Picasso continued painting until his death at 92. Comedian George Burns was making people laugh in his nineties and lived to see 100. So did Bob Hope. Grandma Moses turned to oil painting at age 78, and continued until her death at 101.

Based on your enthusiasm, energy, skills, accomplishments, mental agility, (and forgetting about false indicators such as gray hair or wrinkles) how old would you think you were right now if you didn't know how old you really were? Then use that age, and conduct yourself accordingly.

Gone are the days when retirement meant being put out to pasture to spend your final days rocking on the front verandah. Retirement today usually means the start of a second career, whether that be starting a business or tearing up the golf courses. People are beginning to recognize that 65 or 70 is no longer old and that it's not unusual to be active into their 90's and beyond.

As *United Technologies* urged in their advertising messages, "Don't go fishing when you retire. Go hunting. Hunt for the chance to do what you've always wanted to do. Then do it!"

Second career executives were an emerging phenomenon of the 1990's. According to the book, *America's Changing Workforce* (*Nuventures Consultants Inc.* 1990): "With more executives having good pension fund benefits, paid mortgages, and children out of school, it is likely that many will *retire* in their 50's and work several years in another endeavor."

Many people are *bursting at the seams* to experience those things that the lack of time, money or opportunity previously denied. With risk now possible, retired executives and others are beginning to *do their own thing*.

Although consultants may claim that we should enjoy our jobs or get one that we find fulfilling, it's frequently not that simple. Some of us may find ourselves locked into jobs for financial reasons, family or peer pressure, lack of qualifications, or outright fear of change or risk. Add to that the fast paced environment of work, and most of us never stop to consider whether we could actually do something else, let alone plan how to do it.

But with *retirement* comes a whole new perspective on life. With the pressures of job responsibilities, financial commitments and lack of time lifted, retirees are free to reflect on personal values, smothered ambitions of the past and dreams for the future. Creativity is unleashed, and retirees become entrepreneurs, consultants, writers, inventors and many become very successful network marketers. They turn to jobs and activities they really enjoy.

They self-actualize. Hobbies become businesses and businesses become hobbies.

George Crone, owner of a gravestone company, claimed that people in the fast lane don't take the time to write their epitaphs anymore. Perhaps if they did, they might be forced to reflect on how they would want to be remembered. And that could lead to new directions and goals.

Although it would be great if everyone would evaluate their lives earlier in their careers, an increasing life expectancy, combined with early retirement, make it possible to fulfill lifelong dreams *after* retirement. James E. Buerger, writing in *Quote* magazine, stated that if a person speaks mainly of the past he is old. If he talks of today, he is middle- aged. But if he is always talking about the future, he is young no matter what the calendar may indicate. Goal setting can help keep us young.

Programming your mind for success

Writing goals down provides commitment. Scheduling activities in your planner that will lead to those goals provides commitment. Sharing your goals with other people provides commitment. But you also need an *attitude* of commitment.

When you have lost weight in accordance with your plan, do you keep your "fat clothes" just in case? When you set a goal of a half-hour of cycling daily, do you simply rent a bike for a week at a time just in case the urge passes? How committed are you to your personal goals?

A necessary ingredient of success in anything is *commitment* to a goal. It takes determination, perseverance, and self-discipline. It isn't easy. But it's even *more* difficult to keep to a plan if you make it easy to cop out. Burn a few bridges behind you. Don't store your cigarettes on a top shelf while you attempt to give up smoking. Don't keep your savings in a jar on your dresser when you're saving towards a vacation. And don't borrow your neighbor's jogging shoes when you decide on a daily workout. Set your goal and commit yourself to it. *Believe* that you will attain it. Be *confident* that you will *maintain* it. And *act* accordingly.

You've probably heard about the power of positive thinking so often that you're sick of it. But it is a necessary ingredient of success. And in spite of our exposure to it - in spite of our *belief* in it - most of us don't practice it. And in most cases *attitude* is the difference between success and failure.

What other resources do we have that are any greater than the next person's? We all have the same number of hours in a day. Our physical abilities are similar in most cases. Among our associates or competitors there is not that much variation in our experience or education. And let's not kid ourselves, our abilities are not that much different either.

The big difference is our attitude. Do we have that *desire* to succeed? Dr. Maxwell Maltz maintained that you may never realize your full potential unless you assume you have it. His simple formula was to assume it's possible, rehearse doing it, and do it!

You must act the way you want to feel. Smile. Take a front seat at sales meetings. Make eye contact with your customers and associates. Visualize success and play the part. Act confident and you'll be confident.

There's nothing mysterious or supernatural about the power of positive thinking. Our motivation to strive towards a goal is determined by our *desire* to reach the goal and the strength of our *belief* that a particular action will lead to the achievement of that goal. This is an accepted theory of motivation. And the *belief* that our efforts will result in achievement is *positive thinking*.

If our belief is strong enough - if we think positively - we will be motivated to work hard towards our goal.

And there's the catch. Don't expect positive thinking by itself to achieve goals. There's effort involved as well. Determination, persistence and self-discipline. You can't *wish* things to happen. You have to *make* them happen. But if you think positively, you will be motivated to work towards your goal in spite of fears and temporary setbacks.

And don't forget; you must *have* goals. Successful people make things happen. But without goals you will not know what it is you *want* to happen.

Attitude is the most important factor in success. And with a positive attitude you will be able to overcome those setbacks. They're not failures. **90% of all failures come from quitting.** Don't quit and you don't fail. The world is filled with people who have succeeded because they refused to quit. Thor Heyerdahl, author of *Kon Tiki* was turned down by 20 publishing houses before his book was finally accepted by Rand McNally. Lawrence Peter's *Peter Principle* was turned down by 17 publishing houses before it was finally accepted. The author of *Little Women* received a letter from a well-known Boston publisher: "Stick to your teaching Miss Alcott. You will never be a writer." Other "rejects" include *The Rise and Fall of the Third Reich, Love Story, The Godfather, Exodus,* and *Chicken Soup for the Soul*.

With a positive attitude you'll remain in control. You won't allow other people to control your emotions and reduce your effectiveness. After all, if someone refuses to buy your product, or criticizes you personally, it's not their refusal or criticism that affects you. It's your *reaction* to their refusal or criticism. Don't allow *others* to control how *you* feel. Take a positive attitude. Think about the dozens or hundreds of people who *buy* your product and *praise* you. And get on with the job of success.

Eliminate the word "try" from your vocabulary. There's no such thing as "trying". There's only doing it or not doing it. Be positive. And *do* it.

Visualize your success

There is the story of a champion bowler who never experienced failure. He claims that as a child his father would set the pins up in the gutter, since that's invariably where he threw the ball. But when he started sending it down the alley, the father set the pins in the alley. There is no doubt that success breeds success, and that visualizing yourself as a success does much to ensure that you do become successful.

Psychology Today back in July of 1985 reported on the use of video playbacks of athletes. David Drazin, a clinical psychologist, created tapes of athletes at their best, winning a race, beating an opponent at tennis or sinking a putt. The videotapes were voiced over with commentary from the athletes describing the sensations and thoughts they had at the time. The athletes watched the tapes immediately before competing to give themselves a boost in self-confidence. According to a study completed by Drazin on the effectiveness of these tapes, golfers who viewed tapes of themselves at their best had the highest scores in putting competitions.

A further example of visualization in action was provided on a cassette tape produced by Jack Kinder, Jr. Two lowest ranked members of a California State tennis team evidently shot to almost instant stardom after participating in a mind-programming process. The tennis players were videotaped every day during practice and all the mistakes and bad shots edited out. The composite tape eventually produced showed the players playing to perfection, making faultless serves, volleys and shots. The tennis players viewed these edited tapes of themselves, and practiced what they saw. Within two weeks they had changed their lives and became undefeated representatives of their college team. By changing the way they viewed themselves, they became successful at what they did.

Bill Glass, during one of his talks, told the story of Jim Brown, who had gained over 200 yards against New York. When asked after the game how he had managed to get himself so "up" to perform the way he did, Jim Brown replied that all week long before the game, he saw himself *in his imagination* doing the job - catching passes, making blocks, end runs reacting to every conceivable situation. And when he did perform well, he wasn't surprised.

Athletes who do well see themselves doing well long before the game. If you *want* to be successful in what you do, you must burn into your mind a picture of what you want to become. Norman Vincent Peale, in his book, *Positive Imaging*, claims there is a tendency in human nature to become precisely what we imagine ourselves to be. It goes further than positive thinking, since you don't merely think about a hoped-for goal, you *visualize* it intensely.

So visualize what you *want* to become. See yourself speaking to an audience of 2000 people who are all in your successline. Visualize in detail. See yourself performing, enrolling heavy hitters, making big sales - and collecting and depositing specific checks. See yourself achieving those goals you set for yourself.

Maintain balance in your life

After having emphasized the importance of goals, commitment, persistence, and positive attitude, we have a final word of caution. Don't allow your goals to blur your perspective on life. Some people become so obsessed with the achievement of a few personal goals that they miss out on everything else that life has to offer.

A story is told of a young man who discovered a valuable coin while crossing a field near his home. He kept his eyes fixed on the ground every time he crossed that field, and within a few weeks he had spotted three such coins, worth thousands of dollars. He started searching the field several times a day; before and after work and frequently at lunch hours. He even feigned illness a few times in order to devote more time to his lucrative hobby. He started bringing a rake with him, and then a shovel. Excitedly he would dig in the areas where he had spotted the original coins. His efforts paid off. After several months of digging in the dirt during every available waking hour, he had amassed over a dozen valuable coins.

He became obsessed with the search. He neglected his wife and family, and eventually was fired from his job due to his excessive absenteeism. But he was soon earning ten times his previous salary through the sale of the precious coins. He devoted all his time in the field, eyes glued to the ground, searching, raking, digging ... amassing a small fortune over the years.

Not once did he pause to look at the beauty around him. His eyes never strayed from the ground. He missed the beautiful sunsets, the trees, the flowers, the people, and the birds. He neglected his family, his friends. When he died, he only knew the world as a tiny field from which to uncover valuable coins. All beauty had escaped him.

Don't be like that wretched miser, whose appetite for riches consumed his life, leaving no time for others. No time for observing the beauty of the world. No time for family and friends. No time to live life to its fullest.

Goals are terrific. They give you a sense of direction and enable you to set priorities so you don't waste your time on unimportant activities. But never let a goal become so all consuming that you block out everything else that life has to offer.

CHAPTER 2

PLAN AND SCHEDULE

No person can be effective without adequate planning. Planning moves things from where they are now to where we want them to be in the future. It translates intention into action. Planning forces us to fill our planners with the activities that reflect our goals in life. It protects us from all those trivial tasks that tend to obscure the important ones. And it prevents crises by foreseeing problem areas in advance and providing a course of action that will avoid them.

Planning ensures results. Many network marketers have multiplied profits by setting aside Friday afternoon to plan their activities for the coming week. Others set aside the first hour of each day for this purpose. Frank Bettger, in *How I Raised Myself from Failure to Success in Selling* claims he didn't succeed until he started planning his days.

Few of us deny that one hour in planning frequently saves three in execution. Yet we still don't have time to plan. And we don't have time to plan because we're caught up in the hectic, time-wasting activities that result from *not* planning. We're trapped in a vicious circle.

If you don't feel you have the time to stop and plan, there's only one solution. **Stop and plan anyway**. Grit your teeth and let the world pass you by for a few hours. You may miss a few important calls, lose a few sales, and antagonize a few people. But in the end you will save more time by planning than you stole in the first place. And your effectiveness will multiply. Schedule at least a half hour for planning each day, two hours for planning each week, and four hours for planning each month. Start with a statement of where you want to be, and work backwards from that goal. Don't start the morning by asking yourself "what do I have to do today?" That will only get you involved in activities. Instead, ask yourself "what is it that I am attempting to accomplish today?" Everything should relate to your long term objectives.

How far in advance you plan depends upon your level in an organization. Cars trying to maneuver in a traffic jam would be analogous to a new distributor, seeing only what lies immediately ahead. A lot of wrong moves are a result of insufficient information - unless guided from above. First-line Managers would parallel traffic helicopters radioing information based on a wider perspective on conditions below. Middle to top rank leaders could be likened to an airplane flying high above the helicopter. A panoramic view of the scene below, surrounding territory, and distant landscapes allows directions for an even better and faster route to the distant destination. Long range planning is a road map to the future.

The further ahead you can plan, the more effective you will be as a manager. But don't neglect short-term performance. You can *plan* long-range, but can't *perform* long-range. And doing is as important as planning. So translate your long-range and short-range plans into immediate activities. Fill your planner with those priority activities which will lead you to your goals. Leave only enough room for those last minute emergencies. At the end of each day, determine whether you accomplished what you had set out to do that morning.

Set deadlines on all tasks. Don't overspend time on less important projects. Keep your mind on the objectives, not the activities. Planning is not just for managers. And it's not just for your business. You only have 24 hours every day to divide between your personal life and your business life.

Budget your time

There's no way you're going to get more time than you have right now. But you can accomplish more and live more fully if you budget the time that you do have.

Determine in advance how much time you want to devote to the various activities in your life, such as work, family, recreation, rest, church, associations, and education. Then schedule blocks of time on a planning calendar for these various activities. Start with family time and recreation, two activities that are frequently neglected by entrepreneurs and others. Block out vacation time on the planner while the planner is still free from other encumbrances. Think out these vacations carefully. Consult your spouse and children. Make commitments. Reserve hotels and transportation. Then schedule professional development days, holidays, time you plan to spend with your family, and other special events. Consult the school calendar, your son's hockey schedule, the local baseball schedule, your city's activity calendar. If there's a long weekend you'd like to spend with the family away from home, block it off and make plans the following week.

Next, determine what educational activities you want to participate in. Is there an evening course at the local college that would aid you professionally, personally, or spiritually? Any full-day seminars, weekend retreats, luncheon meetings? Block off the time on your planner, mark them, and then make the necessary arrangements to attend. Do you belong to any associations or would joining one aid in your development? If so, and there's still room on your planner to do it justice, mark it in there.

Next comes the "work" part of your life. But first, a comment or two. The order in which you block off the above activities is determined by the priority that you place on the various activities in your life. If you don't have a family, or if you feel education is more important, you would not plot them in the same sequence. Because there will be conflicts. You can't attend school or church on a day you have set aside for traveling with the family, or vice versa. So it's important that you determine your priorities right at the start. This takes some soul searching. But once you've done it, don't compromise. Or you'll compromise your family and others right out of your life.

Remember that priorities are not always business-related. When pinpointing those important, meaningful activities, be sure to look at your total life.

Determine your priorities

We don't know how long we have to live. It could be decades, years or hours from now. The only time we really have is the time we are spending this very minute. How would you like to spend the last hour of your life? In prayer? With your family and loved ones? Helping others? Watching TV? Reading? Writing a report? Sitting in a meeting? Daydreaming?

Think about it for a minute. Have you picked an activity or two that is so important to you that you would spend the last hour of your life doing it? Okay, good. Now when is the last time you performed that activity? And when is the next time you plan to do it?

You may find that you're not really spending much time on the most important activity of your life. We all tend to procrastinate on the important, meaningful activities in our lives. If this is true in your case, try something. You can always start where you left off later. But right now, spend a few minutes or an hour on something really meaningful to you. Phone your spouse. Or take your son or daughter to lunch. Or visit that hospitalized friend of yours. Or write a poem. Or pray. Whatever is top priority in your life, do it. Just in case you don't get another chance. Then schedule that same activity or activities into your planning calendar every day, week or month for the balance of the year. Make a commitment now to do it on a regular basis. Because, unless you plan to do it by scheduling a specific time for it, it probably won't get done.

The danger of "To-do" lists

"To do" lists are no substitute for planning and scheduling. A traditional "to do" list scatters your efforts over a myriad of tasks. Your energy is dissipated; although much work is done, little of value is accomplished. *To Do* lists grow as time passes. The few important things that you feel you would like to do as the new year starts, soon expand as the year progresses. Like a snowball rolling downhill, daily "to do" lists pick up more and more jobs that you discover as the days go on. Soon the original few priorities are buried among these newcomers, many of which are urgent and require immediate attention. Your original few are seldom urgent, since they were the result of deliberations before the new year began - before you were caught up in the **tyranny of the urgent**.

As a result they are "temporarily" set aside again and again. Frequently they are dropped from the list altogether, since it's a pain trying to keep track of things that will obviously not be accomplished anyway. That's why New Year resolutions are seldom fulfilled. The intentions are good, but the commitment is missing.

Translating goals into activities

The *Taylor Planner*, available from www.taylorintime.com, was designed to enable its user to continue to focus on those original priority goals throughout the year. There is a single page near the front of the planner for the current year's goals. Here you list those goals that you want to accomplish during the year. Not the routine jobs. Not those obligations that do little to further your own success. Only those key projects that you would like to complete. (Exhibit 1)

They could be the ones you have been putting off year after year because you simply haven't had the time. These goals could be personal as well as business oriented. They could include the writing of a book, a trip to Europe, or achieving a higher rank within your company.

In order to determine the target date (recorded in the column to the right of the goal), estimate how many hours it would take to complete the task. This is impossible to determine accurately. Simply guess, and then add 50% to be on the safe side. For example, if you feel it could take 100 hours of solid writing to finish a book, make it 150 hours. Then divide this figure by the number of weeks you plan to work that year. For example, if you work 50 weeks, then the number of hours each week that you will have to work on your goal-related activity would be three. Since it is difficult to work steadily for three hours on any activity, break this into two sessions of one-and-a-half hours each. To accomplish your goal of writing a book, you would have to spend one-and-a-half-hours twice per week in order to complete it by the end of the year. If this amount of time is unrealistic, set the goal for the end of the following year and work half as long each week. Don't be impatient; be realistic.

Let's assume you have set a goal, recorded the target date, and have estimated that you would have to spend two blocks of time (of one and a half hours) each week throughout the year. Turning to the planner pages, you will find a box at the top left heading "This Week's Priority" (Exhibit 2). Here you record the goal you plan to work towards that week. For instance, "write a book" or "sponsor 3 new distributors" or "promote out a new manager". You will note there is a "Weekly Action Items" column below the "Priority" section on the planning pages for your routine list of things to do. Your priority, goal-oriented tasks and projects are *not* to be included on a *To Do* list. They are to be scheduled directly into the planner pages in specific time slots.

The continual recording of your major goals on each weekly page turns your original intentions into commitments. Each week you must now schedule an actual time in your weekly planner to work on that particular task. Treat these blocks of time as though they

were appointments with important people. In fact they *are.* They are appointments with *yourself.* By now you will already have appointments, meetings, etc., scheduled in your planner. You will have to work around these. But once your priority goal time has been scheduled, resist any temptation to use this time for less important "spur of the moment" things. Imagine they are appointments with your surgeon. Few people would delay life-saving surgery.

This method of actually determining the amount of time it will take to accomplish a goal forces you to be realistic. If you had ten goals, for instance, all requiring two hours each week to accomplish, it is unlikely you would be able to steal 20 hours each week to work on those special projects. You would have no time for your regular jobs (or for family time if you planned to work on them in the evening). But there is always next year. Boil those goals down to the few really meaningful accomplishments which would give you the greatest reward. The reward could be extrinsic (money, promotion, etc.) or intrinsic (sense of accomplishment, satisfaction, etc.).

If you don't want to use a *Taylor Planner,* don't let that stop you. Use a separate piece of paper for your goals, glue it into your planner, and schedule blocks of time each week to work on those goals. (You must have a planner that breaks each day into time segments, however. Little blank squares for the days will not work.) Your planner is your most important time management tool, so choose it carefully. If you prefer to work with an electronic planner, that's fine. But it must be portable and easily accessible.

Eliminate New Year's resolutions next year and replace them with a few meaningful goals. Get them into writing, and transfer them into your planner. Then schedule time each week to work on activities that will lead you to those goals. Concentrate your efforts on those few relevant tasks each week.

A magnifying glass will focus the sun's energy onto one spot, burning holes in objects and causing combustible materials to burst into flame. Similarly goals will focus your energy onto a few major activities, magnifying the value of your results.

Using the Taylor Planner

The most important tool for planning and scheduling *is* your planning calendar. But it is equally important that you use it as it is intended, not simply as an appointment book. Here is a summary of additional things to keep in mind when using your *Taylor Planner*. These instructions can be adapted to apply to other week-at-one-glance planners as well.

Assuming you have recorded your goals in the *Goals* section of the planner and scheduled the real priorities into the planner, list those important but brief tasks that you would like to get done on specific days. These will include phone calls to make. Spread these minor tasks throughout the week. Be realistic or you will find yourself copying the same tasks into the next day's section.

EXHIBIT 1

Your Annual Goals

In the space below, write in your personal and/or corporate mission statement and list the major accomplishments you wish to achieve during the year, along with the target dates.

Each week, enter into the "This Week's Priority" section of your Planner those goals you plan to work towards that week.

Then, in specific, daily time slots, schedule time to work on those goal-related activities.

As you reach each annual goal, check it off in the left hand margin.

MISSION STATEMENT

√	ANNUAL GOALS	Target Date

© Copyright **Harold Taylor Time Consultants Ltd. 10661 Chinguacousy Rd Box 70044 Brampton ON L7A 0N5 (905)970-0955 info@TaylorInTime.com www.TaylorInTime.com**

When listing people to phone, record the phone number at the same time; it saves looking it up later.

If you have a follow-up file (sometimes referred to as a 1 to 31 file, tickler file, or bring - forward file), mark "FF" in the daily *Follow-ups* section corresponding to the day you plan to follow up a letter, report, assignment, etc. This will remind you to look into the follow up file. A follow-up file is an excellent way of keeping material off your desk until it's time to work on it. Whenever you schedule a task in your planner, be sure to place the related paperwork in the corresponding follow-up file.

Don't forget to record your personal commitments in the planner as well- those hockey games, theatre nights, dinners, etc. Make a note of them in the evening section. Be sure to record time and place of any social events, sports activities, or meetings. Don't keep two planners or you'll be trying to be in two places at the same time. If someone needs to know where you are, and what you have scheduled, photocopy your week's plan and leave a copy with them.

Carry a sheet of self-adhesive colored labels in the front pocket, and flag important events such as birthdays, conferences, doctors' appointments, etc. At the end of the year, you can use your current planner for reference and mark those same recurring dates in next year's planner. It's almost impossible to miss an important date when a bright red dot screams out at you from the page. You can use different colors to differentiate between birthdays of family members, major clients, team members etc. Place the labels in the daily *follow-ups* sections.

Stick a small pad of yellow sticky notes on the inside front cover (use about a third of the pad to reduce the bulk). They come in handy. When a customer asks you to follow up on something or call him or her with some information as soon as you get back to your office, write a reminder on a sticky note and stick it on top of a scheduled task in your planner. You can't possibly forget. **In** fact, you won't be able to see what you have scheduled in that time slot until you *have* removed the sticky note.

Keep an emergency supply of business cards in the card pockets at the front of the planner. Use the back pocket to store stamps, labels, blank checks, or other items used on a regular basis.

Record conference dates, meetings, holidays, business trips, etc., that are scheduled a year or more in advance on the calendars provided for future years (near the back of the planner) Don't ignore them simply because they're "way in the future". You may need that information at any time. When you get next year's planning calendar, schedule them into it immediately, along with more detail. *Make sure you order your next year's planner no later than October of the current year.*

When scheduling meetings, trips, conferences or other events in the daily section, record as much information as necessary, including flight numbers and times, addresses, hotel confirmation numbers, and even instructions on how to get there. Little hand-sketched maps come in handy if you have to return to the same place at some future date.

Retain all your past year's planners. You may want to refer to the information in subsequent years. It's amazing how we tend to forget those places we visited, people we met, things we did, etc. Who knows, you may use them to write your autobiography some day! And, if you ever get audited, perish the thought, they provide an accurate record of how and where you incurred expenses.

The *Taylor Planner* has perforated corners at the bottom of the right hand pages so you can open your planner to the current week. Be sure to tear off the corner at the end of each week.

Use the *General Information* page near the front of the planner to record that essential information that you need with you at all times, such as frequent flyer numbers, club membership numbers, etc. Also be sure to take the time to enter your name, address and telephone number in the "Personal Information" section. Treat your planner as though it were your wallet; once it's being used properly, it's a lot more valuable.

Keeping interruptions to a minimum

If you have developed some clear-cut annual goals, broken them down into weekly activities, and scheduled those activities in your planning calendar, you are well on the road to managing your time successfully. But you still have to do the actual work. And one of the most common complaints of business builders is the number of interruptions throughout the day by unscheduled visitors. They don't resent the real emergencies - after all, that's part of their job. But most drop-ins are simply delivering some paperwork, or asking a question which could have waited until later, or making a social call.

There's nothing wrong with being friendly. But there is a time and a place for everything, and friendships rarely develop when one of the parties has been interrupted during a priority task that has a fast-approaching deadline. You have just as much right to resist such interruptions as an airline pilot does in the process of landing his or her craft. Pilots are not interrupted because they are intent on the job, cabin door closed. Everyone realizes that what they are doing is important. They also realize they will be available later for conversation.

If you want to be effective, you will have to be more like an airline pilot. Don't be afraid to close your door while working on certain tasks. Focus on your job. And let people know when you will be available. If you have an assistant, these "quiet hours" are easier to obtain. You can have your telephone calls and visitors intercepted for you, and your assistant can

Exhibit 2

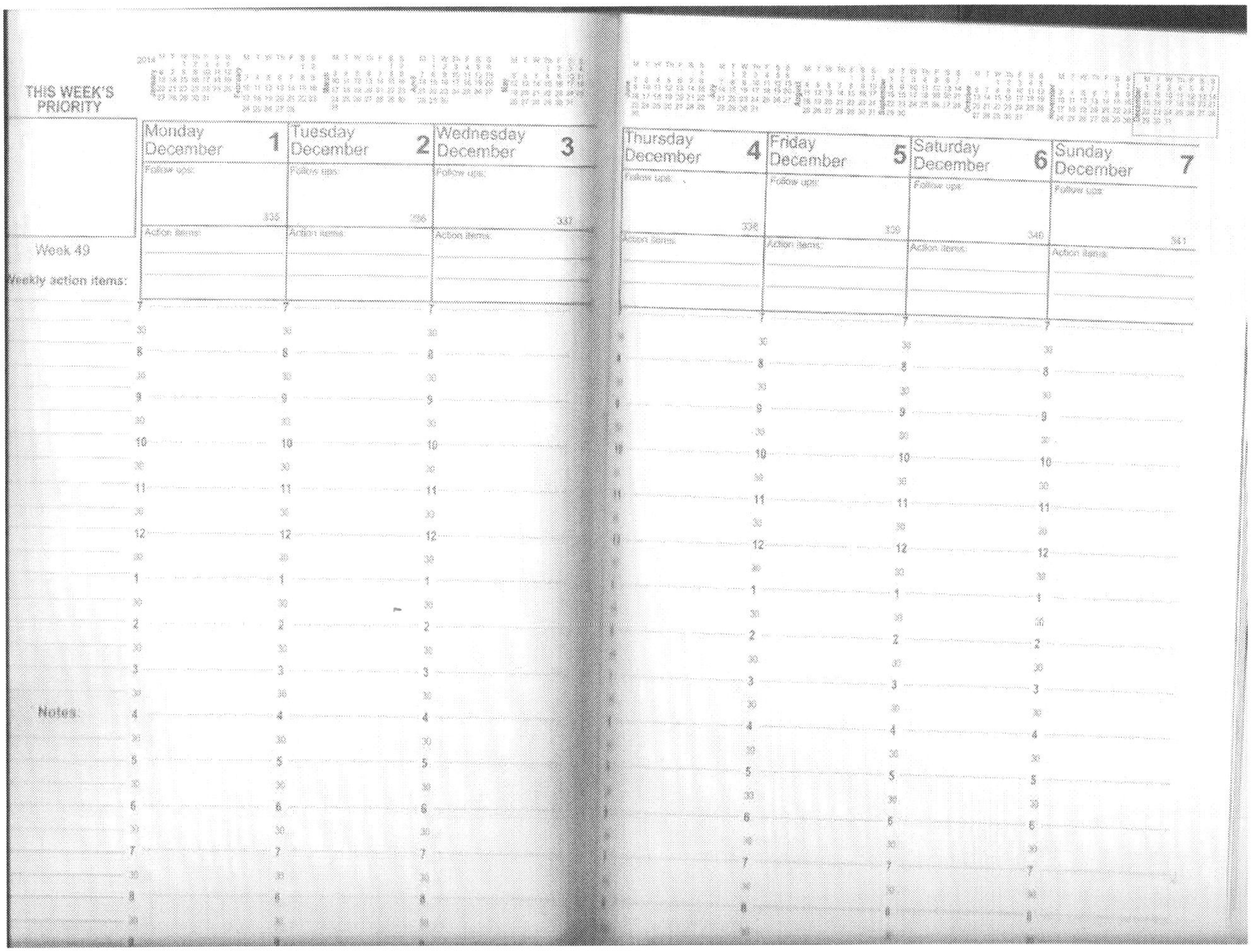
THIS WEEK'S PRIORITY

Week 49

Weekly action items:

Notes:

Monday December 1 — Follow ups: — 335 — Action items:

Tuesday December 2 — Follow ups: — 336 — Action items:

Wednesday December 3 — Follow ups: — 337 — Action items:

Thursday December 4 — Follow ups: — 338 — Action items:

Friday December 5 — Follow ups: — 339 — Action items:

Saturday December 6 — Follow ups: — 340 — Action items:

Sunday December 7 — Follow ups: — 341 — Action items:

keep people advised as to when you will be available. If you are on your own, you may have to resort to a voice mail and a sign on your closed door. There may still be the odd "break-in" but there are few emergencies that cannot wait an hour or more. You may require two or three of these "quiet hour" periods each day. And you shouldn't have to start work early or stay extra late at night in order to have them.

Your door will still be open during the greater part of the day, and you will be more prone to those trivial interruptions during this time. It's important not to *look* interruptible. Don't have your desk facing the open doorway so everyone walking by catches your eye. Have a pen in your hand even if you're just reading a memo (it's important to highlight important sentences anyway). Concentrate on what you're doing. You know you're busy, but everyone else doesn't. So act the part. When listening on the telephone, make notes so drop-ins won't think you're available for conversation with *them* as well. Don't look up at the sound of shuffling feet or rattling paper. If you are still in an office job-until your new business really takes off, you will know that most office prowlers will not interrupt someone's work without a little encouragement. In chapter nine, dealing with technology, you will learn ways to prevent interruptions through modern electronic means.

To discourage people from entering your office, keep your in-basket *outside* your door. (This will also discourage you from interrupting *yourself* every time a deposit is made in your in-basket). Only have one chair in your office if that's usually all you need. And you might try leaving your computer bag or jacket there to discourage people from sitting down. Visitors tend to flop on impulse - even though they've been sitting all day. If you need more chairs, keep them a fair distance from your desk - far enough away to make them awkward to use.

You can also prevent uninvited guests from using the chairs by standing up when they approach your desk. They will not sit down while you're standing, and stand-up conversations don't last long. But don't stoop to these gimmicks unless it's absolutely necessary. If you do decide to visit with someone, be polite, but businesslike. Don't automatically offer your guest coffee. They frequently accept it just to be agreeable. And coffee-sipping drags out conversations.

Don't hesitate to set a deadline on any unscheduled interruption. Communicate clearly. "Yes, I'd like to discuss that right now too, Sam. Can we cover it okay in ten minutes? I have an urgent matter that I have to get back to then." Similarly, don't hesitate to put the person off until later if you don't have the time right then. "I'm really under the gun right now, Sam. Could we discuss that a little later this afternoon?"

If you do decide to talk to a visitor when he or she drops in, don't be afraid to end the conversation when you have finished the business. Use a conversation closer such as, "Well, I appreciated you drawing this to my attention, Sam. I'll get on it first thing in the morning." Stand up as you close, for added emphasis.

If these spontaneous meetings seem to drag out, take a good look at *yourself.* Are the conversations revolving around *you?* Few of us are too busy to talk about ourselves. Concentrate on determining the visitors' needs, take care of it, and then urge them on their way. Managers need all the time they can get to work undisturbed on their priority tasks and projects. And curbing those drop-in visitors is a sure way of increasing effectiveness.

Stacking activities

We all have certain obligations that can only be performed in the evening. But try to stack your meetings and other obligations on the same evening, in order to keep some of your week nights free. For example, you might have one committee meet over a light dinner consisting of sandwiches, your church committee meet from 7:00 p.m. to 8:30 p.m., and your trade association committee meet from 9:00 p.m. to 10:30 p.m. The longer in advance you plan these meetings, the more realistic this option becomes. It only takes one meeting to tie up an entire evening. Stacking meetings provides *ending* times as well as starting times, and ensures more productive use of time.

Summary

If you want to be effective tomorrow you will have to plan today. Here's a summary of what we have suggested to date:

Step 1: *Set lifetime goals*
Things don't "just happen." Success requires conscious effort. It results from achieving goals that you set for yourself. So be sure to set some specific lifetime goals, and then break them down into simpler short-range goals. Don't be discouraged by the magnitude of some of the tasks that have to be accomplished in order to achieve your lifetime goals. Remember that a successful life is simply a series of successful days. And a lifetime goal is reached by achieving a series of short-range goals.

Step 2: *Set daily goals*
Make sure you have daily objectives. Don't look at today as an extension of yesterday. Look at it as an independent unit of time. Set daily goals that tie into your weekly, monthly and annual goals. Judge your performance on a daily basis. Before you leave each night, determine whether you accomplished what you set out to do that morning.

Step 3: *Schedule wisely*
When scheduling priority tasks, always block off time early in the week. Then, if something more important crops up, or you run out of time, you'll have a second chance at it during that same week. If you're at your peak in the mornings, *schedule the priority tasks early while your energy level is still high.* Protect that early morning "prime time" from mundane tasks and interruptions. And don't forget to schedule more time than you think you'll actually need.

Step 4: *Question your activities*
Everyone talks about working on "priorities". But how can you tell which activities are priorities and which aren't? Priorities relate to goals. You must first have (in writing) goals you want to achieve. If performing a specific activity will help achieve those goals, it's a priority. Goals can be personal as well as organizational. They may involve self- development, spiritual growth, and health, as well as business results, expansion and improvements in your ability to service your clients. In order to determine whether you are working on priorities and not spinning your wheels on "filler" activities, ask yourself the following questions:

- Is what I am doing now leading me closer to my short-term and long-term goals?
- What would happen if I didn't do this task?
- By working on this task, am I putting my time to the best possible use?

Step 5: *Accumulate small tasks*
Don't work on brief activities sporadically throughout the day. Accumulate an hour's worth of those brief jobs like telephone calls, memos, letters, etc., and get them done at one sitting. Close your door, have visitors and telephone calls intercepted, and go at it.

You will get more done in less time with this scheduled "quiet hour" than you would if you pecked away at them during the day.

Step 6: *Don't keep separate lists*
If people stopped writing long lists of things to do, they'd have more time to do them. Whenever you think of something important that you have to do, jot it directly into your planning calendar on the day or week that you plan to do it. Schedule the important tasks at a specific time in the day, and protect that time from interruptions. Writing things on separate lists does nothing to further their accomplishment; scheduling a specific time to complete them is a commitment to get them done. If the items are relatively unimportant, or can be accomplished in a few minutes, jot them in your daily *Action List* column or on your weekly *Things to do* column in your time planner, not in a specific time slot. But don't keep separate lists of *Things to do*.

Step 7: *Use prime time wisely*
Most people report that their prime time is early in the morning. They feel at their peak full of energy and enthusiasm - ready to take on the world. Then their enthusiasm and energy wanes as they experience the day's crises, problems and setbacks.

If you have more energy in the mornings, reserve that time for your priority tasks, whether they be sales presentations, writing, training, or budget preparation. Schedule those things that relate to your main work objectives early in the day. Even if the rest of the day is fragmented by interruptions, telephone calls, meetings and rush jobs, you will at least have accomplished the important high pay-off tasks. And you are more likely to do a good job.

Never leave important items until later in the day simply because you feel there may be more time later. Time always seems to dissipate faster as the day goes on. It's better to start a job and not complete it that day than never to start it at all. If a task is going to take about ten hours to complete, consider scheduling an hour or two at a time over a period of two weeks.

CHAPTER 3

WRITE THINGS DOWN

Time is lost, money wasted, problems created, and tempers primed - all because of a reluctance or neglect on the part of people to write things down. Most people overestimate their memories and underestimate their busyness. And they discover, too late, that their intentions had been lost in the heat of the battle.

After all, how could we remember to carry out that directive when we had to immediately reach for a ringing telephone? And no wonder we forgot to follow up on that telephone request with two people simultaneously bursting into our office! We hop from one task to another, dozens of thoughts spinning in our minds. When a new thought occurs we frequently interrupt what we're working on to pursue it before it escapes us. We're constantly juggling tasks and interrupting our staff. Occasionally people jot things down; but on scraps of paper, cigarette packages, and *To Do* lists which get lost in the shuffle.

To be effective we must be organized, and this involves a system of recording that will eliminate the need to interrupt our team members or the task at hand and prevent us from forgetting those messages, directives, and ideas that rain upon us.

Telephone & Visitor's Log

There are two major categories of follow-ups that tend to fall through the cracks; those received via the telephone or personal visits and those that we think of ourselves - those ideas that pop into our heads when we least expect them. For the first category, draw up a "Telephone and Visitor's Log" form. Keep it simple, with space for the name, company, and telephone number of the caller. Divide the sheet into two vertical columns labeled "Nature of Business" and "Action Required". Every time you answer the phone or receive a visitor, quickly jot the information into this log, summarizing the key points on the left side and using the right side only when action is required as a result of the call. Even if the phone rings incessantly or a steady stream of visitors invades your office, you won't forget to follow up on anything. It's all there, in writing. When you have completed the task, cross out the notation on the right side of the log. A quick scan of the pages will tell you whether there's anything left undone. If you prefer, you can purchase ready-made forms at www.taylorintime.com.

Try it. Keep these forms in a binder on your desk. Have it opened at the day's date ready for action. When you make or receive a call, automatically pull the binder in front of you and, instead of doodling on a scrap of paper as you talk, make notes in the *Nature of Business* area. You will be recording information that you may need in the future, even though you may not realize it at the time. When the person at the other end of the line makes a request, jot it down in the *Action Required* area. Record the name and company of the caller at the start or during a pause in the conversation. Before you hang up, be sure to get the phone number, even if you already have it in your directory.

It only takes a second for the person to give it; it could take ten times that long for you to look it up.

If you receive your messages from a mobile device when you are travelling, take time to record the important aspects of the call as soon after the calls ends as possible. This may mean that you need to pull your car over and jot down the details or perhaps record them verbally in the voice memos feature in your cell phone. We will discuss this at greater length in chapter nine.

Now you have a good back-up system. You can relate who called, when, about what, and the nature of the action requested - even months later. Can your memory do that? If requests or even the phone calls have ever slipped your mind this is not a time saver, it is a *must.*

The form shown in Exhibit 3 has space to indicate whether the telephone call was initiated by yourself or the other party, the length of the call, and the time the call was made or received. This additional information allows you to determine the time of the day when most calls are received so you can schedule your quiet hours, lunch hours, breaks, etc. accordingly. It also flags the long-winded callers, or tells you that you are spending excessive time talking to certain individuals. You may find, as many people do, that 80 percent of your telephone time is spent talking to 20 percent of your callers.

This Telephone and Visitor's Log can protect your back as well. People tend to have short memories. They feel they have been waiting "weeks" for materials they had requested only a few days before. A typical experience might be as follows:

> "Harold, I just received fifty brochures in the mail. I asked for 100, and that was about two weeks ago!"
>
> *"Oh, I thought you had only asked for fifty. And it didn't seem that long ago."*
>
> "No, it was 100", he might insist, "and it was *at least* two weeks ago when I called you."
>
> *"I'm sorry, you're probably right. I have a terrible memory. Just a second, I'll check it out".*
> (While talking, I would flip the pages until I came to his call.)
> "Oh, here it is. No, the call was made last Tuesday, Sam. And you did ask for 100 originally. But it's crossed out. Something about not including your successline members in this distribution ... "
>
> "Oh, that's right, I forgot about that. And it was only last week?!"
>
> *"Yes, Tuesday, February 19th. "* (a pause)
>
> "What do you do, record all your calls?" (he might ask)

"Yes, I do. I want to make sure nothing falls through the cracks."

Those may not be the exact words, but let it be known that you make notes. It's for their benefit primarily. But it also discourages them from exaggerating or distorting the truth a little. And it's amazing how they tend *not* to exaggerate in the future!

It's embarrassing (and sometimes costly) to forget what you promised a person during a previous conversation. Or that you even *had* a previous conversation. Some people, who now use a telephone log, claim they used to forget the name of the person before they even finished the conversation! Now, since the name is the first thing recorded, they are never embarrassed by not being able to recall the person's name at the end of the call.

Although the *Telephone & Visitor's Log* (Exhibit 3) prevents embarrassment and "protects your back", it is primarily intended to eliminate some of those time wasters caused by forgetfulness or lack of concentration or failure to listen. It's difficult *not* to listen when you are actually making notes on what is being said. And there's less likelihood that you'll be distracted by visitors walking into your office. There's an almost irresistible tendency to try to carry on two conversations at once - one conversation consisting mainly of hand motions to a drop in visitor. If someone walks into your office uninvited while you're on the phone, ignore that person. The caller was there first. Just keep making notes until the call is finished.

Use this *Telephone & Visitor's Log* for both incoming and outgoing calls. In the latter case you can jot down the items you wish to discuss in that left-hand section and check them off as you discuss them. This way, nothing will be forgotten and you won't have to make a second call. If the person is not in when you call and you leave a message to call you back at a specific time, write "to call back between 3 and 4" in that "Action Required" section. This will act as a flag in the event that the person doesn't call back as requested. Some people don't return calls promptly - if at all- especially if it's information that *you* want. You may want to call again if you need the information before a certain date. How many times have you left a message, never received a call-back, and *forgot* to follow up? When you call again and reach your party, simply cross off that "to call back" notation and away you go.

The same form can be used when someone drops into your office (by invitation hopefully). Making a note of the request can only impress the visitor with your obvious intention of following it up.

This all sounds very easy. But be careful. You may find you "forget" to use the log. Or it gets put away somewhere. Or it's not opened and you can't be bothered going through the hassle of recording what will probably be a brief call. It takes persistence. Force yourself to use it for a week. The second week it will become easier. Soon after that it will become a habit. And remember, habits are hard to break - even the good ones!

The form you use is not important; the important thing is that you *use* it. You could even use a simple steno pad. Draw a vertical line two-thirds of the way across the page, do your note-taking on the left side of the line, and record any actions required as a result of the call on the right side of the line. Or you could purchase a *Telephone and Visitor's Log* (Exhibit 3) from Harold Taylor Time Consultants Ltd.

The end result of this form should be to take action, not just to remember. Don't allow those follow-ups to sit on your form for long. Do them, schedule a time to do them in your planner, assign them to someone else, or add them to that list of things to accomplish tomorrow. Throw out most of the forms once you have extracted any needed information, such as telephone numbers, address, etc. Some of the forms, containing key information could be filed chronologically for future reference. But don't allow them to build up indefinitely.

It's not only important to write things down, but to do it in an organized manner. Develop the habit of recording your calls, visits, delegations, and other ideas that occur. This form, combined with a daily planning calendar, will keep you from overlooking, misplacing or forgetting ideas, tasks and assignments that would put a strain on your effectiveness.

The Telephone & Visitor's Log placed in a binder with other relevant forms, will become part of your "Personal Organizer".

Telephone Directory

Many people still keep business cards, even though they are quickly outdated and difficult to organize. Some people have a desk drawer filled with them, and think they're organized if they have them divided into piles with elastic bands around them! Can you imagine trying to find a specific card? They would play "search and find" every time they wanted to retrieve one. Then, once they had used it (unsuccessfully in many cases because people are always changing jobs), they would toss it back in the drawer and would waste more time later.

To eliminate this hassle, use a PDA (cell phone, tablet, etc.) for your contacts or draw up a directory form. By adding a set of alphabetical tabs to the Personal Organizer, these sheets could be included in any quantity. If you run out of space under the 'A's or 'B's you need only add more sheets. If the directory becomes outdated you only have to copy over one page at a time. The telephone directory is always with you when you're talking on the telephone. Numbers can be transferred easily from the Telephone & Visitor's Log to the *Telephone Directory*. An example of the *Telephone Directory* is shown as Exhibit 4.

EXHIBIT 3

TELEPHONE & VISITORS LOG

NAME _____ **DATE** _____

COMPANY _____ **TIME** _____

NUMBER _____

NATURE OF BUSINESS

- CALL ☐
- VISIT ☐
- INITIATED BY:
- MYSELF ☐
- OTHER PARTY ☐
- TIME: _____

ACTION REQUIRED

LENGTH OF CALL MINUTES

NAME _____ **DATE** _____

COMPANY _____ **TIME** _____

NUMBER _____

NATURE OF BUSINESS

- CALL ☐
- VISIT ☐
- INITIATED BY:
- MYSELF ☐
- OTHER PARTY ☐
- TIME: _____

ACTION REQUIRED

LENGTH OF CALL MINUTES

EXHIBIT 4

TAYLOR Telephone Directory

NAME / ORGANIZATION / ADDRESS	OTHER	CONTACT NUMBERS

taylorintime.com

EXHIBIT 5

MEETING PARTICIPANTS ACTION SHEET

NAME OF GROUP: _____ DATE: _____

IN ATTENDANCE: _____

AGENDA ITEM	DECISION REACHED	ACTION REQUIRED	PERSON RESPONSIBLE	COMPLETION DATE

Meeting Participant's Action Sheet

If you attend meetings, this is another key area for note taking. Use a pre-printed "Meeting Participant's Action Sheet" to summarize the decisions reached, action required, whose responsibility it is to initiate the action, and the date that action is to be completed. With this summary sheet you won't have to wait for the minutes to arrive before you take action. You will also be able to spot any errors in minutes. And if there are no minutes, these notes are a must (Exhibit 5).

The "Meeting Participant's Action Sheet" will also enable you to keep the meeting on track even though you are not the chairperson. If you find the group discussing an agenda item before a decision was reached on a previous item, you can break in with "Excuse me, Jack, I didn't hear the decision reached on the previous item." Groups frequently drift to other items inadvertently, and you can quickly bring this to their attention. A study conducted by R.M. Greene and Associates revealed that approximately 35 percent of topics discussed at meetings did not terminate in any action outcome. By being an active participant, you can help make the meeting more effective. If you have taken the time to attend the meeting, you owe it to yourself - and to others - to help make the meeting as productive as possible. Make sure you get your money's worth, because meetings are expensive.

By filling in the columns of the "Meeting Participant's Action Sheet" you can quickly tell whether any essential decisions were made (or not), what action is to be taken, the person responsible, and the date of completion. Ideally, everyone at the meeting should keep similar notes.

Don't rely on your memory

If you have ever forgotten to follow up on assignments or commitments you have made, have interrupted your successline or family several times a day, failed to take note of a phone number or had a telephone request "slip your mind", develop a Personal Organizer. You will eliminate a handful of time wasters. Don't rely on your memory and don't resort to scraps of paper. Make notes in an organized manner.

Get in the habit of writing things down. If you don't feel comfortable using an electronic handheld device, carry a small scratch pad or several index cards in your pocket or purse at all times. If you meet someone at a dinner party or get a brainwave while watching a soccer game, you can capture the idea immediately. And don't forget to make maximum use of your time planner. Write as much information as possible in it, including names, addresses, phone numbers, locations, cities, hotels, materials required at meetings, flight numbers, restaurants visited. Enter special events such as birthdays, anniversaries, weddings. Flag them with small colored self-adhesive labels. Record those necessary but low priority "things to do" in the appropriate column. When you record a reminder to call someone, include the telephone number so it's easier to follow through later. Draw maps of how to get to meetings that are located at unfamiliar locations. Jot down expenses and mileage. The more information you are able to record, the more useful your time planner will be when you want to recall where you've been, who you met, what you did, and how much you spent.

Writing things down increases your ability to concentrate as well as aids recall. Make notes at seminars and when attempting to commit something to memory. Read with a highlighter in your hand and a pen within reach. Mark key words and passages, make marginal notes for later review. Never rely on your memory no matter how good you think it may be. Jot notes on incoming mail as thoughts occur to you. Write notations on the backs of business cards at the time that they're given to you. Make notes when listening to audio recordings or watching a DVD. And keeping a diary or daily log is a terrific idea.

It's difficult to take notes while you're driving, but you can do just that if you get yourself a hands-free digital recorder or a cell phone with one built in. If you're listening to a CD, for instance, simply stop the player when an idea strikes and record the thought. But don't do anything that would distract you from your driving. Choose your time and place to do any recording.

Away from the business

The habit of writing things down should not be confined to work. You can save time and frustration if you apply the same principles at home. Here are a few examples of how writing things down can keep you organized in the home:

Mark important dates, professional development days, birthdays, holidays, etc., on a wall calendar visible to the whole family. As another special day becomes known, (field trip at school, church meeting, etc.) record it immediately.

Post a "needed" list on the refrigerator or kitchen wall and ask everyone in the family to record items that you run out of- such as peanut butter, soap, toothpaste, salt, lunch bags, etc. Then you won't miss anything when you go shopping.

Keep photocopies of family members' birth certificates on file. You may need them if your children enroll in competitive sports, private schools, etc.

If you are in the habit of ordering items by mail without keeping back-up copies, at least jot the name, address and phone number of the company on the back of the check or print out and save a hard copy of the online receipt. If you're afraid you might forget you *ordered* something, jot a reminder in your planning calendar a few weeks into the future along with the phone number. If you haven't heard from them by then, you might want to give them a call.

Develop a checklist to use whenever leaving for a weekend or longer. For example:

- adjust thermostat
- give key to neighbor
- advise relatives of itinerary
and so on.

If you continually refer to the same dozen or so recipes in a cookbook, you can save time by clipping out those well-used recipes and pasting them on 3 x 5 index cards. If you don't want to mutilate the cookbook, photocopy the appropriate pages. Do the same with recipes from magazines and newspapers. A card file is easier to refer to than a folder full of clippings - and much easier than continually thumbing through a cookbook.

When moving, don't leave all the packing until the last minute. Start packing a few cartons at a time at least a month before the move. Label them as to contents and where you want them to go. Develop a checklist of things to do before, during, and after the move - everything from booking the mover to connecting the new telephone.

Use your planning calendar at home as well as for your business. Make sure it's large enough to allow scheduling of tasks in specific time slots. Once you make up your mind to get a specific job done, or take the children to a movie, or play tennis with your spouse, schedule it directly into your planning calendar.

Plan ahead to eliminate time-consuming trips to the cleaners, hairdresser, shoe repair, post office, hardware store, department store, etc. Keep a list with you at all times. Add any items you need as you think of it. Then make one trip only to the shopping mall, dropping into the different stores and crossing the items off your list as you get them.

For planning meal preparation, make up a form listing the days - Monday, Tuesday, etc., and plan the whole week's menu. Make sure you have all the items necessary a week in advance. Three or four weeks' menus will provide enough variety - simply number them Menu 1, Menu 2, etc., and repeat them. Keep them on a clipboard or fasten them to the fridge with a magnet. If your spouse or children get home from work first, they can get things started. By rotating the menus so the current one is always on top, the whole family will know what is planned.

Everyone is aware of the importance of writing things down at school. Good note-taking can make the difference between a pass and a failure. Similarly, in all other areas of your life, writing things down in an organized manner can help you to be an effective manager of time. So whether in school, at work, at home, or in a classroom, there's no substitute for writing things down. Work at it. Make it a habit. And your effectiveness will soar.

CHAPTER 4

DON'T PROCRASTINATE

Leonard A. Paris wrote the following ditty entitled "Procrastination":

I've gone for a drink and sharpened my pencils,
Searched through my desk for forgotten utensils,
Reset my watch and adjusted my chair,
Loosened my tie and straightened my hair,
Filled my pen and tested the blotter,
Gone for another drink of water,
Adjusted the calendar, raised the blinds,
Sorted erasers of different kinds,
Now, down to work I can finally sit . Oops!
Too late, it's time to quit!

Sound familiar? It happens to the best of us. Procrastination is truly the thief of time. It robs us of valuable time, frustrates us, and forces us to respond to everything on a crisis basis. It's so easy to pick up the procrastination habit. It's easy to rationalize the delay. And we substitute activities such as shuffling paperwork, straightening our desk, sorting through the mail or engaging in idle conversation. Procrastination is a parasite, eating away at our effectiveness. We must understand why and *how* it operates and then eliminate it.

Procrastinators are not rare. People in our time management seminars have consistently rated procrastination as one of their major time problems. There is even a *Procrastinator's Club of America* that boasts over 4000 members. And that doesn't count the half-million members who haven't got around to paying their dues yet! An article in the *St. Petersburg Times* announced that Les Waas, elected president in 1956, still holds that office, since the association hasn't held their 1957 elections yet. Another article from a different publication explained the association's difficulty in selecting the "Procrastinator of the Year". To quote, "The nominating committee never gets around to suggesting any names. They share the belief that if anything is really worth doing, it's worth putting off."

Although operating in a light vain, this Philadelphia-based Club actually exists. We wrote for information, and after a 2 ½ month delay received a reply which opened with "Dear Fellow Procrastinator: Please forgive our sending the enclosed application for membership so few weeks after your request, but all of a sudden our work got all caught up and there was nothing else left for us to do. (These things happen.)" That was twenty years ago and we have yet to return the form. I'm sure that qualifies me for membership.

Although many people make jokes about procrastination, it is more than an annoying habit. It can actually stifle our success, happiness, and in some cases, our very lives.

How we procrastinate

Most of us never become what we could have been. And the main reason for this is procrastination. We put off taking that college course, or starting that business, or developing that idea for a new product, or beginning the first chapter of that book that we want to write. The reason most of us put off starting a major task is the magnitude of the task itself. Four years of study and sacrifice and work is such a long time to spend at college. Developing that new product will take months and months. We would have to learn about patents and rights, accountants, search out interested companies; spend weeks researching the market, countless hours refining the product. And that book! To produce 250 typed pages of publishable material is overwhelming in itself. Then comes the editing and re-writing, the contacting of publishers, the endless correspondence.

We intend to do it. But such a monumental task warrants being delayed a little. So we put it off until the weekend. But we're invited to someone's cottage on the weekend, and that's so much more enticing than hunching over a keyboard or straining our eyes in a library. And even though we don't feel well enough the following weekend to start the project, we are still excited about it, and we actually discuss our ideas with other people.

Other people's enthusiasm mingles with our own and we are more resolved than ever to get started at it. But since it's a big task and we want to do it right, we decide to put if off until the summer. Then we can spend weeks on it! We can work outside on the patio. The children will be at summer camp. Distractions will be minimal. We have rationalized our first major "put-off".

Unfortunately, there is some unexpected illness in the summer, and our friends from out of town come to visit, and that opportunity to tour the Rockies ... we conclude that a major undertaking such as this has to be planned well in advance. It makes more sense to leave it until the kids are married. But who could have foreseen the time demands of married children, what with the grandchildren and frequent visits. Not to mention those extended holidays in Florida now that we have earned four weeks' vacation. And the housework seems to take as long as ever-probably due to those baby-sitting marathons with the grandchildren. One thing's certain. When we *retire,* there'll be plenty of time to write books and develop products and get into your own little business. And there's nothing unusual about senior citizens attending college ...

But now that retirement is upon us, and we have earned the right to relax, our enthusiasm fades. And our legs bother us now, and it's hard to concentrate on a manuscript with this gnawing backache. The doctor agrees that a warmer climate would be better for us, although the heat seems to sap our energy. There's such a need for volunteers, the work at the church seems to be increasing, and it's hard to turn down an opportunity to play bridge when there are so few pleasures left in life. Our spouse is bedridden, and so demanding.

We envy those people who are rich and famous and happy. Jack Wilson, three doors down, wrote three best sellers. Sally Botham just sold her cosmetics firm for over two million dollars. We knew her in school and she sure didn't start her business with brains. She must have married a millionaire. Bill Bridges actually made the cover of MacLean's Magazine. Don't know why, he never looked much when *we* knew him!

If *they're* successful, think how successful we would have been, if only we'd had the opportunity. But what with getting married at nineteen, and raising four kids, and being uprooted from our home every four years … we just didn't have time to capitalize on all our talents.

We spend our time during retirement reflecting on what could have been, making excuses for our lack of achievement, and feeling sorry for ourselves. "It's too late to start now", we reason, "We'll probably be dead in another five years."

And if we're *not* dead in another five years we can kill the balance of our life by playing the "if only" game. One thing's certain; we can't put off dying.

The scenario just painted is all too common. During a "phone in" radio show in Miami recently, one elderly gentleman told us he had always wanted to build grandfather clocks as a hobby. Frustrated by a lack of time he finally promised himself that he'd start once he retired from his full-time job. Well, he'd been retired for over eight years at that point, and still hadn't gotten around to working on that hobby he loved so much.

What is procrastination?

It's sad. But many people procrastinate their lives away. In this larger context, *procrastination can be defined as putting off what you want **most** for what you want **at the moment**.* We say we want to lose ten pounds, for example. That's what we want most. But that yummy looking piece of chocolate cake – that's what we want at the moment. And those momentary wants usually win out.

Why do we put things off? We realize that the present is all we have – that tomorrow may be too late. We are also aware that putting off today's tasks simply adds to tomorrow's burdens. And none of us wants to be one of those people who spend their whole life preparing to live and never getting around to enjoying each moment as it comes. And yet we procrastinate. Why?

Well, first we have to understand what procrastination really is. Some things have to be delayed; others should be delayed. But if we continually put off doing high priority activities by doing low priority activities instead, we are procrastinating. We straighten our desk, sharpen our pencils, and empty the wastebasket, instead of writing that letter to Aunt Sally. We sweep the sidewalk; putter in the garden, smooth the kinks out of the garden hose, instead of taking the kids on an excursion to Wonderland. We thumb through magazines, read the paper, watch TV, instead of getting started on that article we've always wanted to write.

Priorities differ from person to person. A kinkless garden hose may be more important to someone than exercise or recreation or family time. But we all know what our own priorities are. They are those **meaningful activities**, which, when completed, bring a sense of **achievement and satisfaction**. They are the activities that help to attain those personal goals and desires that burn within us.

It is amazing how adept we are at thinking of other things to do when facing an important task. You would think that we would be enthusiastic about an activity that would produce gain, satisfaction, achievement. But unfortunately the satisfaction is not immediate. The gain is not always something we can readily perceive. And is the achievement not something that can be delayed – so we can delay the unpleasantness of the moment? There's the catch. Few things worthwhile come without effort, inconvenience, or discomfort. Our natural tendency is to avoid unpleasantness. So we sacrifice long-term benefits in favor of those minor, short-term rewards.

It's only natural to want to relax after dinner instead of washing dishes, even though the delayed task will be even more difficult after the food stains have been allowed to harden. And who could fault us for leaving the broken stair unrepaired until after the football game, even though it presents a safety hazard? And sleeping in on Sunday morning requires less effort than taking the family to church. There is always a diversion at hand to make shirking our responsibility to others and ourselves more palatable.

Sometimes procrastination has minor consequences. At other times, it results in death, injury, or unfulfilled lives. There is even the odd time that procrastination produces favorable results (and oh, how we love to rationalize our habit by recalling those occasions). But the habit of procrastination, regardless of the results, is self-defeating in the long run. It makes us feel guilty because we realize it's wrong. It's debilitating, because we're constantly dreading the task being postponed. We're more tired mentally by not doing something than we would be physically if we were to do it.

The activity we are postponing could be unpleasant in itself, such as weeding the garden if that's an activity that we deem unpleasant. Or its *magnitude* could be unpleasant. An activity such as writing a book, for example, could be *overwhelming* if we dwell on the length of time it would take. We tend to put off tasks that are either unpleasant for us, such as writing statistical reports, doing the laundry, or making a sales call – or those that will take an overwhelming length of time, such as saving $5000 for a trip to Europe, finishing a recreation room, or writing a novel.

Overcoming procrastination

To overcome the habit of procrastination, we must generate some enthusiasm to offset the unpleasantness. We must concentrate, not on the activity, but on the **reward** awaiting us upon completion. If the activity is unpleasant, let us pounce on it immediately and complete it so we won't have to dwell on its unpleasantness. If it's an overwhelming activity, let us chop it up into manageable chunks and polish it off a piece at a time. If we have to drive to the other coast, let's aim at driving six hours each day. If we have to write a book, let's aim at completing six typewritten pages each day. If we have to pack the contents of a house in preparation for moving, let's aim at packing six cartons each day.

The hardest part of any job is starting it. It requires great effort to get a loaded wheelbarrow in motion, but once moving, it tends to stay in motion. We are a lot like that wheelbarrow. Let's resolve to get started and let our momentum carry us on. Let's not wait for better conditions, a more suitable time, or better equipment. And let's not kid ourselves into thinking we need inspiration to do anything creative. An English music critic, Ernest Newman, is claimed to have said that the greatest composer does not sit down to work because he's inspired, but becomes inspired because he is working.

Author Ari Kiev once wrote, "When you postpone your involvement in something, you will probably never accomplish it, and you will be left with memories of past wishes rather than past deeds." Yesterday will never come again, and tomorrow may never arrive; but today is ours. That's why it's called the "present". Let's make the most of it.

Procrastination is really just a state of mind. We tend to look at jobs in their entirety and are overwhelmed by their magnitude. For example, if we want to write a 300-page manuscript, we visualize 300 pages of typewritten words and are immediately convinced of the hopelessness of the situation. By sheer willpower we finally start, and after what seems a painfully long period of time, complete 10 pages. Now the situation seems even more hopeless when we compare those meager 10 pages with the 290 pages yet to be done. We are shocked into inactivity.

The solution is *not* to look ahead at the 300 pages that we must fill with words. If we do, it is the same effect as looking down when we are walking across a narrow bridge 10,000 feet above a chasm. A narrow bridge only 10 feet above a chasm is not as fearful. Similarly, only 30 pages of material is not as fearful. So make *that* your goal.

Break the large, overwhelming task down into ten manageable tasks of 30 pages each. Look ahead only at your *first* task, start right in, measure progress against this new target, and amazingly, you won't become discouraged. In fact, after 15 pages, you will delight in the fact that you're already half-way to your first goal of 30 pages.

Only when you have reached your first goal of 30 typewritten pages do you allow yourself to think about the *second* goal. You dig right in, and before you know it, the second goal has been reached. Now, even if your mind jumps ahead and thinks about those eight more goals to be reached, it is not as discouraging. In fact, you now *know* that you have reached two goals without much difficulty. There is no reason to think you cannot reach the other goals in the same way.

The more you do, the more motivated you get, and by the time you have reached the halfway mark in attaining your ten 30-page goals, the momentum has really built up. The last goals will be achieved much faster than the first ones.

This process of breaking seemingly impossible tasks into manageable goals can be applied to almost anything, whether it's completing a degree course at college, saving enough money to buy a house, or wallpapering ten rooms. But since procrastination is a state of mind, you must ensure that your mind zeros in on the immediate goal at hand and does not dwell on the one overwhelming objective. You can do this by putting your goal in writing, and blocking out specific times in your planning calendar to work on it. So if your first goal is to complete thirty pages, write on an index card or in your planner:

"Goal 1: Complete 30 pages of copyl for 'How to stop procrastinating' book by December 30th."

If you use a card, carry this card with you in your wallet or purse. Or tack it on the wall above your desk. Or stick it on your mirror in the bathroom. Put it somewhere where you will see it and read it every day. If you have a Taylor Planner, enter it on the "Annual Goals" page and take your planner with you when you travel. Then estimate how much time you will have to spend each day or week to write those 30 pages. Assuming there are 15 weeks available between the time you start and the December 30th target date, you will need to write 2 pages each week. If it is realistic to write one page in an hour (and always allow more time than you think is necessary) you should schedule two hours each week into your planning calendar. So you might block off between 8:00 a.m. and 9:00 a.m. every Tuesday and Thursday. This will prevent you from scheduling appointments or other activities in those time slots. You will also be committing yourself to sit down and write at 8:00 a.m. every Tuesday and Thursday whether you feel like it or not. Be sure to allow for those interruptions as discussed in the chapter on planning.

Protect those one-hour work sessions at any cost. If there is something truly critical that must preempt that time, then reschedule your writing time later that day or the following day. But always spend two hours per week writing. It will soon become a habit, like brushing your teeth each morning, or doing your daily exercises.

Is there some task that you want to accomplish that you have been putting off until you have more time? Well, the time is now. You have twenty-four hours every day. Are you willing to trade one of those hours for something really meaningful to yourself and your family? Then do it. Stop procrastinating.

Five step action plan

An action plan to reduce procrastination can be summarized in five steps.

Step 1. Recognize that you do procrastinate.

We normally think of procrastination as the act of putting off a task until later. But it also involves *giving precedence to a low-priority task.* You may be engaged in performing a necessary task, but if you are doing so at the expense of a more important one, you are procrastinating. If you are going to lick procrastination, you will have to recognize when this is happening. This is not as easy as it sounds since procrastination, for most of us, has become a habit. We tend to put off unpleasant tasks without even realizing we are doing so. It's an involuntary reaction that most of us fall prey to. Since habits are actions we take *unconsciously,* the first step is to be *aware* that we are procrastinating. If you don't admit that you procrastinate, you will certainly never cure it.

Step 2. Make up your mind that starting today you will break the procrastination habit.

You must *want* to change. It is possible, with effort, to break a bad habit by replacing it with a good habit. But breaking the procrastination habit is not easy. It involves a lot of self-discipline. And self-discipline is *doing something that doesn't come naturally.* For example, if you have been getting up at 7:30 am. Every day for the last fifteen years, it's not natural to get up at 6:30 a.m. You have to set the alarm and then *make yourself get up.* It's hard work. But eventually you will form a new habit. And a habit is something you do naturally. The same thing applies to going on a diet, engaging in a regular fitness program, giving up three cups of coffee and a morning newspaper, leaving the TV set turned off after dinner, *doing something now instead of leaving it 'til later.*

So much is dependent upon self-discipline, that if you are really serious about gaining control of your time, you're going to have to face one fact: initially, it's *hard work.* And no timesaving gimmicks, ideas, or systems will change that fact.

So the next time you are about to toss something aside until later, stop and ask yourself "Would it be better to do it *now* and get it over with?" If the answer is "yes", make up your mind to do it. If the answer is "no" because there are more important things that need doing, schedule a specific time in the *future* to do it. Break the habit of procrastination by *consciously deciding a course of action on every job.* Eventually a new habit will be formed – the "do it now" habit of consciously deciding whether to do an activity as it arises or to schedule it for a later period.

Step 3. Pick one of those tasks that you have been delaying, regardless of its magnitude, and block off at least one hour in this week's planning calendar to work on that task.

Treat it as you would an appointment with a very influential person such as your boss! Resist the urge to displace the "appointment" with other urgent matters that arise. It should be scheduled in ink. Commit yourself to keeping that appointment with yourself to work on the task.

Step 4. Work on it at the scheduled time regardless of how tempting those more pleasant diversions may be.

If you can isolate yourself from interruptions during this brief period of time, so much the better. If it is impossible to prevent interruptions, be sure to schedule more time than you think the task will require. In other words, *allow* for those interruptions. Each time the interruption is over, resume the task immediately.

Step 5. Continue to work on improvement.

If you have followed the above steps you will be surprised at how much you actually get accomplished, and that it wasn't such an overwhelming or distasteful task after all.

If you have the time, continue to work on it while the momentum is strong. But if you have run out of time, schedule another block of time in the future, and repeat the process. Any task can be accomplished, regardless of how overwhelming it may seem, if you persistently chip away at it.

We procrastinate because of the magnitude or the unpleasantness of the task. In a way, we are afraid of it, so we delay starting it. But nothing is as difficult as it seems. Once we get a piece of it completed, we have a sense of accomplishment which motivates us to continue plugging away at it. When asked, "How can we ever feed one million starving people?" someone replied, "One at a time." It's this one bite at a time persistence that accomplishes great things.

Dr. Donald and Eleanor Laird, in their book, *The Technique of Getting Things Done,* emphasize the importance of doing **first** those things you hate the most: "The doer likes his work because he has no unpleasant jobs hanging fire. He has already cleaned them up. He does not dread the next task, for the unpleasant task is behind him."

We all procrastinate at times. But if you find yourself straightening your desk or sharpening pencils or grabbing a coffee, ask yourself whether you are not just delaying the start of an unpleasant task. If you are, muster all the willpower at your disposal and get the "*do it now*" habit. If those unpleasant tasks are also *important,* do them first and get them over with. You'll be surprised how much time this "*do it now*" habit will save.

51

Get an early start

If you have made up your mind you are going to develop the "*do it now*" habit, start the moment you wake up in the morning.

The effectiveness of your day can be predicted within the first hour. If you get off to a bad start – if you're disorganized, prone to procrastination, vulnerable to interruptions – then your day will probably follow suit. But if you are organized; if you have a daily goal, a plan and productive work habits, you will accomplish much.

Since the early hours of the morning are critical to the success of the day, the time to prepare your plan for those early hours is the afternoon or evening before. Don't leave the office until you have organized your desk and listed your objectives for the following day. Schedule the activities in your daily planner. Clear your desk except for anything needed to work on those first priority jobs. Resist the temptation to just walk away from the mess at quitting time. Chances are, if you're disorganized when you leave at night, you'll be disorganized when you return the next morning. Psychologists have concluded that managers who leave the office with a clear idea of what they want to accomplish the next day, actually enjoy their personal lives more that evening. In contrast, those who leave with their desks and minds in a muddle, enjoy themselves less.

Try getting up earlier in the morning. You may be sleeping eight or more hours each night out of habit. If you need it, fine. But experiment first. If you sleep a half hour less each night you'll gain an extra week each year. But more important, you'll get an early start on the day. You'll have time to review your day's plans. And ask yourself whether what you had planned that day will really lead you closer to your goals. You'll also have time to change these plans if circumstances have changed in the meantime.

Don't start the day with activity. Though many of us are action-oriented, dying to get into the thick of things – "doing" instead of thinking – the greatest productivity gains are made not by doing more work, but by eliminating unnecessary work. We must look before we leap. Getting to work early, ahead of the other people allows us the opportunity to select the real priorities of the day – and to get them done before other people even start theirs.

There's a proverb that tells us "As the first hour of the day goes, so goes our day." Believe it. Don't allow yourself to procrastinate at this crucial period of the day. The temptation is great because the real priority tasks are often the most difficult, time-consuming or distasteful. Take a lesson from the child who eats his spinach first to get it over with and then thoroughly enjoys the rest of his meal. Dig right in to the arduous task and get it over with. Most of us have a tendency to delay that first early-morning task. We use coffee and greeting rituals as our excuse. Or the morning newspaper. Or email.

Realize that the longer you delay something the more pressure you'll be working under and the more things there are that can go wrong.

Build up some early morning momentum and you'll be able to coast through the day with less difficulty. Physics tells us that an object at rest tends to stay at rest. The same law applies to human endeavor. Overcome your daily inertia with a burst of early morning enthusiasm. Once you get rolling, you can plow through those daily tasks and achieve your daily objectives.

But above all, make sure you *have* daily objectives. Don't look at today as an extension of yesterday. Look upon it as an independent unit of time. Set daily goals that tie into your weekly, monthly and annual goals. Judge your performance on a daily basis. Before you leave each night determine whether you accomplished what you set out to do that morning.

Get organized. Set goals. Plan each day. Get up early. Don't get sidetracked. Dig right in to that priority task. Review accomplishments. If you can do this on a continual basis, you will have no trouble getting started in the mornings.

Bonnie McCullough, in her book, *Totally Organized,* says she makes her bed the moment she gets up, even before going to the bathroom. She claims she's not so tempted to go back to sleep, and no doubt that neatly made bed gives her a psychological lift and gets her on the way to a productive morning.

Getting an early start isn't always easy. The bed is so comfortable and warm, and the alarm clock is viewed as an intruder to be silenced with a swipe of the hand. But if you can overcome that initial stage of inertia by forcing yourself to swing out of bed and onto your feet, the next time it is easier. Soon it becomes a habit. Early risers tend to get more done. The early hours of the morning contain fewer interruptions. Telephones are silent. Children, depending on their ages, are either asleep or trying to compensate for those silent telephones. But if you are an "early person" and can function effectively at 6 a.m., you can easily get a jump on most people.

A word of caution: getting up early and simply wasting this prime time on extra long showers, third cups of coffee and yesterday's news does not make for good time management. Schedule *at least one* priority task to be accomplished each morning. Some people write books by simply writing at the kitchen table for one hour each morning. Others beat the traffic by going in to the office for a quiet hour each morning. Others, whose family consists of "early persons", use this opportunity for quality time with the family. It can be productive time. But it's a choice. Will lingering in bed justify things left undone? And remember, procrastination is giving up what you want most for what you want at the moment. Think about it.

Make a commitment to act

Although procrastination is an insidious timewaster that should be eliminated, don't be too hard on yourself. Usually it's the busiest people who are the biggest procrastinators. They simply try to do too much. Unfortunately with so many irons in the fire, there's a danger of delaying the wrong things.

If you have a heavy workload, make sure you prioritize your activities, and delay those items that are low on your list. If you have too long a list, consider eliminating or delegating some activities.

To ensure a commitment to actually *perform* a task, remember to schedule it into a specific time slot in your planning calendar; don't leave it sitting on a list of "Things to do". There is little commitment in a "to do" list.

You may be confused as to when delaying is procrastination and when it is not. Reviewing the section on goal-setting and prioritizing should clarify this, since you should never postpone a priority. Rarely should you delay the following:

- Situations involving your family
- Thank you's, either verbally or in writing
- Expressions of sympathy, concern, congratulations, etc.
- Problems requiring your attention
- Decisions that must be made

In general, it is always better to act quickly as opposed to putting off the inevitable. Delaying a decision is like writing a check to cover an overdrawn account. It does not solve the problem and yet could make the situation even worse.

In her book, *Creative Procrastination,* Freida Porat defines negative procrastination as those idle and unplanned uses of time which block us from achieving a more fulfilled life. Positive or creative procrastination, on the other hand, denotes time that is deliberately *planned and scheduled* for our own use. If you delay a task by scheduling a time to do it at a later date, that's *creative* procrastination. Providing you actually *do* it at that time. But if you delay a task with the idea of doing it *sometime* later on, that's *negative* procrastination. It's important to distinguish between the two.

We started this discussion with a poem entitled "Procrastination". Here's another one with the same title. The author is unknown.

> *There's a loving letter, I mean to send*
> *There's a visit, I mean to pay,*
> *There's a careless habit, I hope to mend,*
> *When I get time, someday.*

*There's a dusty Bible, I mean to read,
There's an hour, I'll keep to pray,
And I'll turn each dream to a golden deed,
When I get time, someday.*

*I'll carry flowers to the sick and sad,
I'll seek for those, who stray,
You may trace my steps by hearts made glad,
When I get time, someday.*

*So we've thought, and so we've said,
Yet, how sad to relate,
That busy with less important things,
We've waited until, too late.*

It's not too late if you start now. There's only one cure for procrastination, and you're it! You must decide right now to take control of your own life. Set goals, determine your priorities, schedule your activities, and develop the *"do it now"* habit.

CHAPTER 5

DON'T BE A PACKRAT

We would never think of hiring people to simply sit at a desk for eight hours per day just in case we need them someday. The waste of money would be unforgivable! Yet we allow "things" to sit around not being utilized, just in case we need them some day. And it costs money. Public storage companies are making big profits because, to quote one of them, "We are a world of savers, and people have to keep hold of things." Many storage companies report rental income of millions of dollars every year.

We are complicating our lives with all the stuff we buy and accumulate. Daniel Pink, in his book, *A Whole New Mind (2006),* points out that self-storage, where people store the stuff they no longer have room for at home, is a $17 billion business. That's larger than the motion picture business. According to the *Self Storage Association*, the number of self-storage facilities has grown about 70 percent in the last decade. And what we don't store, we just throw away. Ciji Ware, in her book, *Rightsizing Your Life*, claims that Americans are known around the world as the major consumers on the planet, generating nearly 200 million tons of household garbage a year. The U.S. spends more on trash bags than 90 other countries spend on *everything*. The cost of the *containers* for our waste is greater than the cost of all goods consumed by nearly half of the world's nations.

Perhaps you aren't paying an outside storage company $2 or more a square foot each month, but you *are* paying something. If you keep things in your office and never use them, you are paying by taking up valuable space that could be used for something else, perhaps something more productive. You may be spending money on storage cabinets, filing cabinets, shelving, etc., that would not be needed if you simply threw things out. You may also be paying people to move these "things" or sort through them, or count them.

Don't be afraid to get rid of something simply because it has "book value". If you can't sell it or give it away, throw it out. An asset is no longer an asset once it has become a liability.

Packrats lose time, money and space

Packrats are compulsive keepers. The things they keep are not necessarily useless but are seldom used. In fact, most of the items are squirreled away out of sight, nullifying any possible usefulness. Time, money and space are consumed needlessly by these superfluous possessions. What possesses these possessors to possess their possessions? There are many reasons, just as there are different types of packrats. One type of packrat not mentioned below is the collector. These specialists accumulate specific items, whether they are ceramic mice figurines, hockey cards or antique books. This could be classed as a hobby, and is not harmful in itself. Unfortunately it can lead to other collections such as buttons, beer cans and pennies, finally regressing to pieces of string, bottle caps and lint from the dryer. Collecting can become a compulsion in itself.

Here are a few common characteristics of packrats in the form of an acronym spelling the word PACKRATS. A few words of explanation and a suggestion or two follows them. In general, packrats:

Put an unrealistic value on their old stuff.

Attempt to retain the past by retaining past treasures.

Comfort themselves with familiar possessions.

Keep for the sake of keeping (keepsakes.)

Rarely part with gifts.

Always rationalize their decision to keep things.

Take pride in their possessions.

Seldom toss things out without prompting.

Put an unrealistic value on their old stuff. Just because something was expensive to buy in the past, doesn't mean it's worth that much now. Most items depreciate rapidly and replacement costs frequently plummet. This is particularly true of electronic equipment. DVD players that we paid $300 for ten years ago can be purchased for $ 35 today.

Attempt to retain the past by retaining past treasures. What's past is past. We can never relive it. Constant reminders of days gone by can prevent us from enjoying the present and anticipating the future. Getting on with life may require cutting ties to the past.

Comfort themselves with familiar possessions. It's natural to resist change; but it's not healthy. Old possessions that have lost their usefulness may not only comfort us but also serve to encourage the status quo. We should not seek comfort in *things* but in *people*.

Keep for the sake of keeping (keepsakes.) What enjoyment could we possibly get from things hidden in closets, stashed in crawl spaces and packed away in cartons? Out of sight, out of mind. We don't enjoy them because we don't even know we *have* them! This is where packrats get their name. *If you haven't missed something in a year, get rid of it.*

Rarely part with gifts. By receiving a gift you are not making a lifetime commitment. A gift simply conveys a message of goodwill, thanks, congratulations, friendship or love. Get rid of the impractical gifts and keep the message in your heart. That's what's important.

Always rationalize their decision to keep things. Ask a packrat why they keep something and they'll give you a good reason – one that's reasonable to *them*, that is. The favorite reason is, "It'll come in handy some day." It's hard to disprove *that* one. Packrats should keep in mind, however, that disorganization, clutter and space problems are a high price to pay for the off chance that the item may be useable in the future.

Take pride in their possessions. This is not true of all packrats, but includes those who believe that whoever dies with the most toys, wins the game of life. Some people measure their value by the value of their valuables. People in this category should base their self-esteem on who they are and not on what they have.

Seldom toss things out without prompting. Packrats are made, not born. They have developed these hoarding habits over the years. Firmly entrenched, these habits are hard to break. It's easier for packrats to change with the encouragement and reassurance of others. Giving them a book probably won't help; they may not get around to reading it; they'll just keep it.

There may be little positive said about packrat tendencies. But if you have an elderly parent or friend who feels comfortable among familiar possessions from the past, it could be a blessing. Don't feel that you have to talk someone out of tossing away things that add stability and comfort to their life. There is a time to keep as well as a time to throw away.

Getting rid of the backlog

In an office environment, in spite of electronic mail and other technological tools for processing communications, people can become so overwhelmed with paperwork and so pressured by time constraints, that they feel it's impossible to keep on top of it all. They become packrats by default.

If you find yourself buried in paperwork, magazines, junk mail; have an overflowing in basket; desk drawer crammed with files, reports and trivia; with stacks of material on your credenza, window ledges and filing cabinets - you will have difficulty coping with current material. You must first get rid of the backlog, and organize yourself so the paperwork will never get ahead of you again.

But first you must clean up your desk, office, and files. Here is a ten-point system for getting rid of your backlog:

1. Block off a three-hour period in your planning calendar. If it's impossible during working hours, schedule it at night or on a weekend.

2. Empty all the desk drawers, ledges, etc, of paperwork. Don't tackle filing cabinets at this stage - only your desk, credenza, and any visible piles of paperwork.

3. Toss all paperwork into three boxes marked "Priority", "Routine", and "Junk Mail". Stack the magazines separately.

4. As you carry out Step 3, quickly scan the material and toss out the obvious garbage.

5. One of the desk drawers should be a file drawer. If not, use a file cabinet drawer that is within reach of your desk. Install hanging folders.

6. Use 13 of the hanging folders, along with 31 manila folders, for a follow-up file. An example is described later. Label the other folders with titles of your major on-going projects. Every hanging file should contain a similarly labeled manila file folder.

7. One or more of your desk drawers will contain "non-paperwork" - miscellaneous paraphernalia and office supplies. Separate those items you actually *use* on a regular basis, and organize them in an organizer tray. Retain in a shallow drawer.

8. Throw out whatever items your willpower will allow. Place the other items in a shoebox; label "Junk Drawer", followed by the date, and stash them away in some dark closet. Chances are you'll never need them again. Out of sight, out of mind, and eventually, out into the garbage.

9. Go through those three boxes, starting with the one labeled "Priority", dealing with each piece of paper as you pick it up. Scrap it, delegate it, do it, or schedule a time to do it later. In the latter case, block off time to do it in your planner, and put the paperwork in the appropriate follow-up file.

10. It is unlikely you will be able to dispense with all the paperwork in 3 hours. Set the boxes aside and dedicate one hour every morning to systematically go through this paperwork until it is all scrapped, done, delegated, or scheduled for a later time.

Reducing the paperwork flow

An article in *Personal Report for the Executive*, published by the *Research Institute of America*, suggested you shouldn't even take the time to scrunch the discards before tossing them into the wastebasket. To quote, "Papers discarded intact take less space, less disposal time, and less energy (especially if your paper ball misses the target). They are also ready for a clean recovery if you need to retrieve any that were thrown out by mistake."

Getting rid of the backlog will do little good if you fail to curtail the ongoing flood of paperwork. According to Dianna Booker in her book, *Cutting Paperwork in the Corporate Culture*, studies indicate that 50 to 70 percent of all working hours are spent on paperwork. This includes preparing, reading, recording, interpreting, filing and maintaining the information. The percentage has probably dropped since the popularity of email, but not as much as might be expected since 60 percent of email is printed as well.

We can't eliminate reading and writing. Nor would we want to. But where there are such large amounts of time being spent on activities, there are usually plenty of opportunities for savings in time and money. Many hints for reducing paperwork and saving time reading and writing will be discussed in this chapter.

If you have ever experienced a broken arm, and it happened to be your writing arm, you probably experienced a reduction in the amount of paperwork you generated. It's amazing what we can eliminate when it's inconvenient to produce it. Many managers actually receive two or more handwritten memos from one person on the same day – in addition to the usual emails. Wouldn't it have been easier to have jotted down a reminder and included everything in the same memo? Most requests are not expected to be responded to on the same day anyway. If they were, they would probably have been handled by telephone.

Resist the urge to write a lot of memos. Accumulate the ideas and write one memo only or make one telephone call or send an email. It will save time for both you and your associates. And it's less painful than breaking an arm.

Yet another example is the number of photocopies we make that are unnecessary. The photocopier is a convenient timesaver, but it is expensive, even excluding the cost of the operation, maintenance and supplies. According to a survey conducted by *Accountemps*, unnecessary photocopies cost American companies more than $2.5 billion a year.

Executives of the 1000 largest U.S. firms estimated that almost 30 percent of photocopies were unnecessary. Another eight percent were for personal use. Combined, these statistics show that almost *two* out of every *five* photocopies made in the average office are unwarranted expenses. So watch this source of excessive paperwork! A more recent statistic claims that 60% of emails are printed as well, adding to the paperwork explosion.

There is also a tendency to clutter your work environment with little scraps of paper from those "From the desk of' pads that we receive as gifts from suppliers. Resist the urge to scribble memos on those scraps of paper. Telephone instead. If necessary, send an email message. Or return the original letter with your notation added. Scraps of paper get lost or misplaced, accumulate, or are simply ignored. And those personalized pads seem to generate more little notes and memos that would not otherwise be sent. It's as though we are compelled to use them up so the printer or other vendor will give us more. After all, they are usually free –

which might account for our reckless abandon in using them.

Scraps of paper, regardless of their formalized appearance, are time wasters when used in excess. Resist the urge. Instead, jot the reminder in your planner or organizer or on your follow-up list.

And go easy with those little sticky notes. There have been complaints from administrative staff that some managers are slapping those little yellow sticky things on everything that pauses in transit. There have been reports of gobs of the little critters stuck together in the bottom of the in basket, all bearing instructions for handling the papers that they were attached to at one time. Some had *not* come loose, simply having slid down on the page so the arrow now pointed out an error where none existed. One frustrated manager had a wall that shed post-it notes every winter.

Sticky notes are not meant to replace staples, thumbtacks or good old-fashioned writing directly on paper. They should not replace memos, verbal instructions, or brief stand-up meetings. They are a useful assist, but don't get carried away. They do come loose with time, shift position when disturbed, and curl under certain conditions. It's even been reported that they make lousy wallpaper.

Use them indiscriminately and they become a timewaster, not the time saver they were meant to be. It is difficult *not* to be a paperwork packrat because of the constant bombardment we receive from all directions.

Coping with the information explosion

Chances are you are doing more reading related to your business and personal interest than ever before. Magazines, journals, business papers, conference proceedings, flow steadily to your desk. Tens of thousands of new books are published each year. Daily newspapers bombard you with 3 or 4 million words each week.

And the information explosion has only just begun. At the rate at which knowledge is growing it is estimated that in 50 years' time, today's knowledge will account for only a small fraction of the total knowledge available at that time. Information is doubling every two years. How can we cope with all this information?

Well, before you rush off to take a speed reading course, remember that *effective reading involves knowing what to read as well as how to read it.* The first step is to establish some method of screening the chaff from the wheat and spending your valuable time on only those articles, books, websites etc. that will help you reach your business and personal goals. Don't be a packrat, and don't keep every book, magazine and report that arrives at your home or office.

A large chunk of time is spent reading magazines. Print magazines, e-mags, and online newsletters are an obvious source of valuable information. But they are also making increasing demands on our time and space. Here is one method of coping with them:

Handling hardcopy magazines

- If a magazine is not providing information that you can use, cancel your subscription or get off the mailing list. There's no such thing as a free magazine. Our time is anything but *free.*
- When you receive a publication, resist the impulse to toss it aside. That kind of procrastination often builds mountains of magazines which end up being bulldozed to a shelf or table or trucked to another executive's desk unread. It takes only a few minutes to glance at the title page, or skim the articles to determine which ones will be relevant to your area of interest.
- If you're the only one who sees the magazine, rip out those articles you've selected and scrap the rest. More than likely though, you'll want to circulate the magazines or in the case of good reference magazines, retain them in your library. In that case, photocopy the articles you want to read.
- File those selected articles in 3-ring binders, appropriately identified. For example, all articles dealing with time management would be placed in one binder, those on sales meetings in another, and so on.
- Now you can leave the actual reading to a scheduled time period. Try to take advantage of idle time by reading during business trips, while waiting in doctors' offices, airports or during periods of relaxation. Read with a "highlighter" pen, marking relevant paragraphs and sentences. Make notes in the margin. This becomes your permanent reference library with no necessity of re-reading articles to find the relevant parts.

Skimming books and other literature

Books should be read with a "highlighter" and marked up as you read. Significant pages can be photocopied or even summarized for inclusion in your reference binders. The same thing goes for newsletters, conference proceedings and other literature. Anything worth reading is worth retaining for future reference - but only those significant parts. Articles you wish to retain from online newsletters and e-mags should be saved in a folder on your computer or printed out and saved in an appropriate file folder.

Speed reading courses have been known to increase reading ability from 200 words per minute to over 800 words per minute without decreasing comprehension. If you feel you could benefit from such a course, by all means take it.

But not until you have organized yourself in a manner which allows you to cope with the information explosion - and to maximize your reading effectiveness, keeping only the essential information on file.

Surfing the Internet

Statistics Canada figures indicate that the more time Canadians spend on the Internet, the less time they tend to spend with family and friends. An article in the *Toronto Star* reported that half of all Canadians 15 years of age or more spent an average 8 hours per week on the Internet the previous year. One in six people spent over 15 hours per week on the Internet. This extra time has to come from somewhere, and according to a survey of 25,000 Canadians, much of this time is at the expense of family time. And that was back in 2001!

We would hazard a guess that the balance of the Internet time comes from sleep time, TV time and leisure time. Although sacrificing TV time might be a worthwhile trade off, sacrificing time in the other areas might not be such a good idea.

The same precautions apply to the Internet as apply to any other media. Make sure you plan your surfing in advance, with an objective in mind. Set a time limit, bookmark the valuable websites and avoid being sidetracked by links that take you away from your objective. Let others know your areas of interest, trade website information, and have an organized electronic filing system to house the relevant information that you download.

Handling junk mail

Magazines, books and other useful literature are not the only culprits that encourage us to become packrats. A lot of other "collectibles", including junk mail, arrive with the morning mail.

Larry J. Sabato, in his article *Mailing for Dollars* (Psychology Today, October 1984, pg. 38), refers to a 1978 survey that showed that 63 percent of the people really look forward to the mail. Even more than they look forward to daily activities such as watching television, hobbies, eating dinner and sleeping! He also mentions another survey that revealed that 75 percent of the people who receive political mailings actually read them.

Contrary to the popular belief that most junk mail ends up in the wastebasket unopened, it doesn't - at least not until it has grabbed your attention and consumed some of your time. To increase the likelihood of your perusing these unsolicited mailings, such ploys are used as personalizing envelopes, "live" stamps, return postage, teaser copy, red ink, creative copy, and a personalized, conversational tone.

Direct-mail consultants spend their time devising new ways of getting you to spend your own time and money on various getting and services offered. Although I don't recommend you throw out all "junk mail" unopened, since much of it may be profitable, you should be selective. If you recognize from the envelope that the product or service is one you don't need or want, discard it unopened. Otherwise, you'll be trapped into sorting through the interesting, colorful inserts that are designed to capture your interest.

It can become very time-consuming when the direct marketers don't take the trouble to eliminate duplication. If you receive two or three identical envelopes from the same mailer, take a minute to scribble "Return to sender" on the unopened envelope. On the duplicates, add the statement "please remove name from mailing list." Or have a self- inking stamp made up that says it for you.

Unsolicited material can be valuable, keep you updated on what's new on the market, and give you some great ideas for increasing productivity in your business. But it is also designed to attract your attention. So spend as little time on it as possible. And don't get in the habit of opening two or three envelopes containing the same literature.

Be ruthless with those you do open. If their value is in doubt at all, scrap them quickly. Resist the urge to read further or hold them over until later. And don't circulate the material to others unless you can see immediate use for it. When you do send materials to others, note exactly what you want done and whether the material should be retained or scrapped.

File material you want to retain - but not in a permanent file system. Place it in a follow up file or idea file for future action. Record the reason you are keeping it. Discard inserts that are unnecessary and staple the other material together. Don't file loose or paper clipped material. On the pre-determined date, review it and take action. Resist the urge to re-file it. If you don't have time to do anything about it or have second thoughts about its value, scrap it. Err on the side of scrapping too much, never too little.

At the office, if you find the junk mail is consuming too much time, and keeping you from the priority items, separate it from the normal correspondence and place it in a folder of its own. Then, regardless of when you review your mail, leave the folder until the end. If you have used up your allocated mail time without having gone through the junk mail, no harm done. Leave it until tomorrow.

You might even leave the folder of junk mail until fifteen minutes before quitting time. You are normally winding down by then, and in no mood for priority tasks that require mental alertness. With only junk mail standing between you and the evening meal or leisure time, you tend not to dawdle over those eye-appealing folders. The secret is to review all junk mail, but do it quickly, without allowing it to infringe on priority time that could be used for priority tasks.

A young lady attending our time management seminar reported using a self-inking stamp announcing "DECEASED". She stamps all unwanted correspondence and returns it to the sender. It no doubt drives creditors to frenzy.

You may not want to follow her example. But one thing you *should* do is reduce the amount of paperwork you initiate. Paperwork breeds more paperwork, so think twice before putting things in writing. A telephone request will generally result in a telephone reply, but send a memo and you'll receive a memo in return. A *Telephone Log* in which you record telephone requests will suffice as a follow-up reminder, should one be necessary.

Handling incoming paperwork

Since we will be covering electronic mail at great length in chapter nine, we will devote our suggestions in this chapter to paper mail.

If you insist on seeing every piece of mail as it arrives, don't allow it to accumulate. Set aside a time each day to go through your mail, then separate it into priority, routine and junk mail. Put the priority items in a red manila folder, the routine items in a yellow one, and the junk mail in a blue one (or pick your favorite colors). The mail should be stacked in that order, with the red folder on top, the blue folder on the bottom - followed by any magazines.

If you never get to the "routine" or "junk mail" folders, you haven't missed much. Add to them the next day.

Schedule enough time each day to dispense with your mail. It could be 15 minutes or half an hour, depending on your experience. Use that time to get rid of the paperwork. If you simply sort through it and set it aside, you'll be buried in no time.

Here are a few suggestions for dispensing with the various items quickly:

Meeting Notices
Record all the pertinent information, such as time, place, topic, in your time planner and *scrap* the notice. Have a planner that's portable and keep it with you wherever you go. If necessary, retain the original notice in your follow-up file and indicate that fact by writing "ff" in your planner for the appropriate date.

Trivial Letters
These are the ones requiring no reply. Note and scrap. Resist the urge to write back if a reply would accomplish nothing. And don't file them.

Important Letters
Reply immediately. Preferably by phone. If it has to be in writing, consider email. Don't yield to the temptation to procrastinate.

Lengthy Letters or Requests
If it's going to take you over twenty minutes to formulate a reply, write a report, or collect

information, schedule it for later. But commit yourself by recording the task in a specific time slot in your planning calendar. Place the back-up material in a follow-up file under the corresponding date. Indicate "ff" beside the insertion.

Magazines
Don't toss them aside. Check the contents page and rip out or photocopy any articles that look worthwhile. Staple and 3-hole punch them and toss them into a folder for reading during idle time. Scrap the magazine or forward it to the next person on the distribution list.

Junk Mail
Many people get good ideas or information from this unsolicited material, so quickly leaf through it. Make notes on anything of interest which you plan to act on, and slip it into an "idea" file. Check this "idea" file once per week and either put your idea into practice, schedule a time to do it, or scrap the material. Don't allow it to accumulate. Your **in-basket** should be an **"action" basket**, not a holding tray for paperwork. Dispense with your mail daily and you won't be always fighting deadlines and getting further and further behind.

Don't keep business cards

Business cards can also add fuel to our packrat tendency. Sometimes we accumulate so many business cards during the day, we have trouble remembering the reason we asked for them, or we have trouble matching the person to the card, to aid your memory, jot something on the card when you receive it. This could be the place or circumstance in which you received the card, or some information about the person, such as home residence, name of the spouse or children, or other personal information mentioned during the conversation. If you are being asked to send something to the person, take the time to jot that fact on the card. Don't rely on your memory or you may end up sending information to the wrong people.

When you go into your office and have taken any necessary follow up action, don't keep the card. Enter the information in your telephone directory if you have need for it, or add the name to a special mailing list. Or scan it into a database. Then toss out the card. Alternatively, if there is a file on that person, you may prefer to staple the card to the file folder. Accumulating a drawer full of business cards only adds to the clutter and tempts you to waste time searching through them later.

Harold S. Geneen, former chief executive of ITT, revealed in his book, *Managing* that after finishing with a set of papers or report, he turned it over to his secretary who automatically threw it away after three months. Drastic? Perhaps. But Geneen claims he never needed anything more than 90 days. And how many of us actually *do* refer to paperwork once it has served its purpose?

Although you can't throw out everything, you could establish a policy for discarding certain categories of paperwork at predetermined times. This would prevent your files from expanding into a time-wasting hodge podge. Some items you may want to discard almost immediately. A few items would be kept permanently.

The important thing is to review all paperwork and consciously make a decision as to when each item should be discarded. Otherwise you will become inundated with paperwork.

An article, "The Permanence of Paper", by Col. (Ret) Leonard Lee written over 20 years ago, claimed that paper use had increased 25% the previous year. Today, it continues to increase. Several years ago, file cabinet sales in the U.S. totaled over a half-billion dollars annually and computers continue to spew out reams of printouts on paper. In the fall of 2006, Xerox, recognizing the massive amounts of paper being used in copier machines, announced plans to launch erasable paper. After a week or two the print on the paper would disappear, making it reusable up to 50 times.

We're still a long way from being a paperless society. And paper presents a time problem in its generation, handling, reading and filing. Ken Zeigler, in his book Getting Organized at Work , (McGraw-Hill, 2005) claims we lose 45 minutes every day, on average, hunting for things on our desks, going through papers and notes. Here is a summary of ways to keep it under control.

1. Indicate "No reply necessary" on as much of your outgoing correspondence as possible. Otherwise you may get a reply whether you want one or not.

2. Before writing memos, ask yourself, "Can this be accomplished verbally?"

3. Purge your files annually. When in doubt, throw it out. Place a "discard date" on it when you file it to make the purging process go faster.

4. Keep copies to a minimum. Cut distribution lists to include only those people who really need the information. If possible, circulate one copy only. Encourage people to scrap their copies by stamping them "Please note and scrap".

5. Use email. It's faster, less formal, and more likely to be discarded after reading.

6. Make it easy for people to get off your mailing list for newsletters etc. Every six months ask them to sign and return a form or card if they want to continue receiving a certain report. If they don't respond, remove their names from the list.

7. Challenge yourself to write brief memos. Ban two-page memos. Encourage yourself to write clear, concise business writing.

8. Dispense with paperwork as it arrives. The longer you keep it, the more you accumulate,

and the longer it takes to sort through it. And it breeds more paperwork in the form of follow-up memos.

9. Try recording lengthy reports on CDs. It would not only eliminate paperwork, but would allow reviewing while commuting.

10. When in doubt, throw it out. File daily. When the item is fresh in your mind you have a better idea of its importance. When the paperwork is no longer familiar, you tend to file "just in case."

11. Transmit information electronically whenever possible.

It's difficult to file or store things in an orderly way when there's so much of it to store. So don't allow it to accumulate. When in doubt, throw it out. Don't be a paperwork packrat.

CHAPTER 6

STORE THINGS IN AN ORDERLY WAY

Christopher Robin, in Winnie the Pooh, explained organization to his friends. "Organizing is what you do before you do something, so that when you do it, it's not all mixed up."

Do you sometimes feel "all mixed up"? Then take a look at your personal organization.

- Is your work environment organized in such a way that you know where everything is?
- Can you retrieve files and materials at a moment's notice? Or are you wasting time and money searching for misplaced objects, shuffling papers, and interrupting yourself to get more supplies?
- Is there duplicated effort in your office?
- Are papers misfiled?
- Are there constant interruptions, or do you have an orderly flow of materials, and a maximum utilization of time You *can* influence your environment to a certain degree, regardless of your position in the organization. And your environment does influence your management of time.

Ever visit a casino in Las Vegas? The environment there actually *encourages* you to spend time and money. Moving sidewalks take you inside (but leaving isn't as convenient). You must pass the gambling casino in order to get to the registration desk. After registering, you have to wind your way through the gaming tables to get to the elevators. You're tempted. And when you start to gamble, it's so easy to continue. The drinks are free. The chairs are comfortable. Air conditioning and loud colors keep you from getting drowsy. There are no clocks on the walls. No windows. You lose track of time. The dealers' payoff in larger denomination chips. You lose more and faster. The chips are only negotiable at that particular casino so you don't readily move to another one. It's easy to buy chips at any table - but you have to find the casino cashier if you want to cash them in. Everything is conducive to the spending of time and money.

Take a lesson from the casinos. Develop an office environment that encourages the *saving* of time and money. If you can influence the layout of your office, do so.

Arrange the desk to ease the work flow. Place office equipment so as to minimize steps, while keeping in mind the possible distractions. Place the storage cabinet so supplies are close at hand. If you need a product storage room, make sure it's easy to locate the various items.

Don't run out of supplies or stationery. Organize the storage so there's a place for everything. Have written procedures for all tasks. Refine them. Simplify them if possible.

Get a large calendar. Record all meetings, conferences, business trips, vacations, important deadlines so you can see at a glance everything that's happening.

Investigate any office equipment or gadgets that may save you time. Cordless headsets allow you to move around while talking. Use the re-dial feature to save precious time dialing. An electronic reminder will prevent you from spending too much time on one task. Voice-activated software and email will speed up correspondence. PDAs, hot synched with your PC will keep you productive on the road. Embrace technology and your effectiveness will increase.

Organize your private office

Make sure your private office is arranged so as to attract a minimum of interruptions. Don't face the open doorway. Have your desk to one side, so people will have to go out of their way to see you. Or have your desk facing away from the doorway. If they are able to catch your eye from outside the office they will be tempted to walk inside and strike up a conversation. For the same reason, avoid having gathering spots outside your office such as coffee or photocopying facilities. One manager reported that the coffee maker was right outside his office door and people would kill time by walking into his office with a cup of coffee in hand, and socializing.

Although the absence of chairs would make unscheduled visitations brief, it would also make *scheduled* meetings inconvenient. But don't have chairs close to your desk or facing you unless you're short of room. They're an open invitation for people to slip into them. Instead, place them about six feet or more from the desk, and have them *facing each other.* The awkwardness of sitting that far away and looking at you over their shoulder should discourage anyone from heading for the chairs. When the drop-in approaches your desk, you can stand, and remain standing until the brief conversation is over. If you want to carry on a lengthy conversation, simply move from your desk to the chairs and carry on the conversation in the open, facing each other, without the barrier of a desk between you.

Have your office decorated tastefully, but simply. A lot of family photos, trophies, certificates, and citations will encourage chit chat. Avoid comfortable sofas unless you plan to sleep in your office. But plants are great, even if you don't garden. Artificial ones consume less time. And a clock is a great reminder of the speed at which time passes; place it where your *visitor* can see it.

Arrange your working tools and furniture closely around your desk area. Don't place frequently used filing cabinets or bookcases on the other side of the room. You should have everything at your fingertips. Have an adequate inventory of felt pens, paperclips, staples, highlight markers, etc., in one of your desk drawers.

Your desk does not have to be large but you must have sufficient working area. The desk is not meant for storage, so keep it clear of paperwork except for projects you are working on. Other projects should be retained in a follow-up file; the bulkier ones can be kept in colored manila folders, clearly identified. These should be kept in hanging files in your desk drawer. If your desk doesn't have a drawer large enough to hold files, I recommend you get one that does. If this is impossible, keep the follow-up file system and project files in a vertical file holder on the top of your desk or in a filing cabinet to the side of your desk.

The use of binders

You may want to keep articles, procedures, job descriptions, policies, product bulletins and anything else that you refer to frequently in three-ring binders. Binders are great for storing articles, newspaper clippings, reports and other information which you want to keep for reference. Here are a few tips for using them:

1. Make sure they are large enough for the amount of material you hope to accumulate on a specific topic. Half-inch or one-inch binders are useless for categories such as *technology* or *time management*. You would have to make up about ten binders within a few years.

2. Don't divide the categories too finely at first or you'll be overrun with binders containing only a few sheets each. *Time Management* may be sufficient in the beginning. When your binder is full, break out the largest sub-category such as *meetings*. When the original binder becomes full again, break out the next largest category, and so on. Your binders will increase in number only as the amount of research material increases.

3. To file newspaper clippings, use a *glue stick* and paste the article on 3-hole paper. Don't keep a separate file folder filled with small newspaper clippings.

4. For larger newspaper articles, you may want to 3-hole punch the original article. But I recommend you photocopy it first and keep the photocopy. It's stronger, and will not fade and become discolored like the original will.

5. When clipping or tearing out articles, be sure to note the source and date on the margin of the article. You may need this when using the information later, either to give credit, seek permission to reprint, or simply to obtain more information. Example, *Canadian Manager Magazine*, August 2014, pg. 60-61.

6. Identify the binders so they can be spotted quickly. Self-adhesive plastic tabs with insert

cards that are available at office supply stores, and keep your library looking neat. Use different colored insert cards - or better still a cartoon or the picture representing the category. For example: a clock for *time management*, a picture of a computer for *computers*, etc. You will be able to identify the binder at a glance. The bookcase or shelf should be within reach. Surround yourself on three sides with your working materials.

Control your environment

Your office should be arranged so that everything is readily accessible. Every time you have to walk out of your for supplies, you risk an extended interruption. So anticipate the envelopes, letterhead, pads, etc., that you will need, and include them in your inventory. If you need an extra cabinet or shelf on the wall near your desk, get one. Have a set of stacking trays on your desk or credenza bearing the names of people who you communicate with on a regular basis. Whenever there is something requiring their attention, jot notes on it and toss it in one of those trays. When you speak with them or meet them you can cover the items you have accumulated.

Don't let your office environment control you. You spend too many hours there to suffer unnecessary inconveniences. If a floor receptacle prevents you from placing your desk where you want it, have the outlet removed. If the door is in the wrong place, change it. If the lighting is poor, add more lights. If the rollers on your chair are worn, replace them. Any costs incurred are one-time costs; the time savings are forever. Experiment with several arrangements until you get the one that works best for you.

Couches are too comfortable and encourage socializing, but chairs placed around a conference table encourage results. Move the telephone so you have your back to the door when using it. This removes the temptation to be distracted by anyone walking into your office. You can't pay attention to two people at the same time.

If you don't *have* an office, do what you can to build privacy into your "territory". Use dividers, bookcases, plants, and filing cabinets to shield yourself from eye contact with other people. Locate your desk away from the main thoroughfare of traffic if possible. Researchers have concluded that privacy encourages job satisfaction and increases performance.

Try to surround yourself with some protection - even if it's only a free-standing divider or two. Aim for good ones. Make sure they're tall enough to prevent people from peering over - and talking over. Try for an inch or more of sound absorbing material on both sides, and a solid centre. Don't leave yourself vulnerable to interruption from everyone who passes your desk.

If you are unable to hide your desk, at least hide your eyes so everyone doesn't feel compelled to talk to you. A strategically placed plant, filing cabinet, or stand-up portrait ought to do the trick. If your eyes meet those of every passerby, you are asking to be interrupted.

Deniece Schofield, in her book *Confessions of a Happily Organized Family,* offered some good advice on storing household items. Here's one that is good for the office as well: "Paperback books waste a lot of space on the standard 12-inch deep bookshelf. Double up and conserve precious space by storing the books two layers deep. In order to see the back row of books, put two 2 x 4's, one on top of the other, on the back of the shelf to function like a stair step. This will raise the back row four inches and enable you to see and choose the book you need."

The use of labels

Colored, self-adhesive labels help keep you organized. In addition to identifying files and specific categories of paperwork, they are useful (in various shapes and sizes) as follows:

- To indicate the front cover on unmarked binders, books, folders, planner, etc. - to tell you which side is "up".

- To identify suitcases, briefcases, and parcels, when there is a danger of getting them mixed up with similar items - excellent for traveling.

- To highlight important dates in your planner, such as birthdays, anniversaries and vacation periods.

- To identify common objects, such as ruler, stapler, 3-hole punch, which have a habit of "wandering" from your desk.

- To differentiate between different activities on a wall calendar. Different shapes could be different clients; different colors could be different types of meetings, locations, etc.

Available in a variety of shapes, sizes and colors, these labels can be purchased at most office supply stores. Carry a few sheets of labels with you in your computer bag or tucked into a pocket of your planning calendar. They'll come in handy.

The follow-up file

A clear desk does not guarantee that you'll be organized. But it helps. If you have a handful of material relating to a project and nowhere to put it, don't leave it on your desk or toss it back into the in basket. Develop a follow-up file. This is *your* personal follow-up file that contains the back-up material for those tasks that you have scheduled in your time planner. Nothing goes into this follow-up file unless a time to complete it has been blocked off in your planner or a notation made in the follow-up section.

The follow-up file system consists of thirteen hanging files marked January, February, etc., and the last one marked "next year". One set of manila folders marked from 1 to 31, corresponding to the days of the month is placed in the current month's hanging folder. If it's the first of the month and you have emptied the day's project papers, move the manila folder to the next month's hanging folder. This follow-up file system is simply an adjunct to your time planner. Your planner contains your work plan. When you arrive in the morning, flip open your planner and see a report scheduled for 9:00 a.m., you know exactly where to look for the back-up papers needed in that day's follow-up file.

If *more* papers are received related to a specific task that is scheduled for a future date, it's a simple matter to find the appropriate follow-up file folder. Simply flip through your time planner to find the date on which that project is scheduled.

For on-going projects such as committee meetings, book manuscripts, and bulky engineering projects, it's not necessary (or advisable) to jam all the back-up material into the follow-up folders. Instead, use colored manila folders bearing the projects' names or titles. Keep them in your right hand desk drawer, along with your follow-up file. Use hanging folders for these project files for easy retrieval. You will soon know that the red folder is "A" project, the green folder the "B" project, and so on.

Keep a clear desk

Once you have cleared your desk, and scheduled the jobs you didn't have to do right away, you're well on your way to being organized. A few hours invested in this initial clean-up will save millions of precious minutes in the future. You will have eliminated some time wasters - shuffling papers, searching for things, distractions, working on trivial items. While you've got the momentum, do a good job of this initial clean-up. Empty those desk drawers, that shelf under your desk, those cluttered bookcases, credenza and filing cabinets.

Muster up enough courage to throw out anything you can't see an immediate use for. Have a place for everything and put everything in its place, within reason. But leave yourself the luxury of one junk drawer for all those U.F.O.'s (Unidentified Funny Objects) you have collected, such as gold plated paperclips, unusual business cards, and your son's hand carved thumbtack holder that you can't bear to part with. You can carry the organization bit a little too far.

No executive or homemaker can do without that single junk drawer. We all need a *little* disorganization somewhere in our lives. And sorting through that junk drawer every six months or so is more fun and more stress-relieving than an executive sandbox.

Once you have cleared your desk and emptied your in-basket, don't dump things back in again. People are tempted to use it as a holding basket for everything pending or puzzling. Don't. The trivial items will obscure the important ones, which soon become urgent. Fight procrastination by looking at it as an *action* basket. Once you have emptied your in-basket, don't leave material on your desk. Scrap it, delegate it, complete it, or put it in your follow-up file for future action.

You'll be tempted to leave material on your desk temporarily, until you have a chance to work on it. Don't. You'll soon have so much temporary storage, it will become permanent clutter. You'll waste time searching for items. The minutes add up to hours. All those unfinished tasks scattered before you will produce anxiety and stress. You'll be tempted to hop from one unfinished job to another. You'll have difficulty concentrating on the task at hand. Messy desks decrease effectiveness. After all, who can plan with all those urgent, unfinished tasks taunting them? A clear desk will give you a psychological lift. You'll look organized, you'll feel organized, and you will *be* organized.

An integral part of your organized work area is your filing system. In spite of the "if in doubt, throw it out" policy, you will have paperwork that you must keep. So you need more than a follow-up file, idea file, and project files.

Personalize your filing system

File your material so it's easy to retrieve. If you feel you will never need to retrieve it, scrap it. Use hanging folders appropriately labeled. Store the actual material in similarly labeled manila folders so you will always return the folder to the right spot. Your hanging folders need never leave the drawer or cabinet. You could file alphabetically according to category, e.g.: Suppliers, A to Z; Administration, A to Z; Buildings and Equipment, A to Z, etc.

Articles, job descriptions, board meeting minutes, newsletters, bulletins, and anything else you refer to frequently could be kept in 3-ring binders. Label them clearly for easy identification; buy self-adhesive insert holders for the spines. Purge your files regularly; resist the urge to buy more filing cabinets.

Brief clippings from newspapers and magazines, one-liners, ideas, could be stuck onto 3 x 5 index cards with a glue stick and filed according to category. You could tie the various files together with a central reference card file. For example, if you arbitrarily assign a number to every piece of paper you file, you could enter this number in the reference file at the same time. This reference file could be categorized by topic, name, etc.

If you read something that you will want to use later, it's generally a good idea to photocopy that page, or write out the idea on a card and file it under the appropriate category. Alternatively, you could jot down the book and page number on an index card and file that in the appropriate spot.

The alpha-numerical file

Streamlined electronic filing systems that handle all your paperwork either scanned or hardcopy are available online. If you do a lot of filing and retrieval it is probably worth the small investment of time and money. But for a small business you might consider a simple alphabetical filing system

A simple filing system that eliminates misfiling, makes retrieval easy, and assures that something retrieved from the files is put back in the same spot again, is the alpha-numerical system. Here, each category has a reference file folder containing a listing of all sub-headings within that category. Each sub-heading is assigned a number, and that number only, not the heading, is marked on the file folders within that category.

For example, assume you have a category title "Publishing". Take a folder, mark the tab with the word "Publishing", and inside that folder tape an 8 1/2 x 11 sheet of lined paper, and head it up "Publishing". Under this heading, list all the sub-categories or sub-headings that you need. Don't bother to list them alphabetically. It's easy to glance down the list later to find the sub-heading you are looking for, as long as the list doesn't go beyond one page in length.

Now assign a number series to this *Publishing* category. If it's 100, mark 100 opposite the word *Publishing* on the index tab of the main reference file folder. Then opposite the sub-headings, assign numbers 101, 102, 103, etc. Next, mark these numbers on a set of file folders, and file the papers in these folders, marking the same number on each piece of paper you file.

For example, if one of your sub-headings is "book clubs" and it had been assigned the number "106", you would mark "106" on the piece of paper to be filed there. When you want to retrieve it from the file later, turn to the reference file folder, glance down the list until you see "book clubs", note the number opposite it, and pull out the appropriate folder. To re-file, simply stick it in the folder bearing the same number that appears on the piece of paper. Misfiling is unlikely, even when dozens of people are using the same files.

With this system it is easy to add, eliminate, or combine categories. Since no titles appear on the individual folders, it is easy to use the numbered folders for other sub-categories if the existing sub-category is eliminated.

The more time spent in filing a piece of correspondence, the less time spent in retrieval. But how often do you have to retrieve something from the files? It may be more economical and faster to set up a simple system based on topic or date. One administrative assistant insists that filing by date is fastest - even for retrieval. She claims her boss is always asking for a letter that he received "about a month ago" or "last January or February". So she has labeled the folders by the month, regardless of the topic or person originating the letter. Set up a system that satisfies *your* needs. And remember, the name of the game is retrieval, not storage.

Hints for effective filing

In spite of regular purging and other paper control strategies, your files will continue to expand. Make it a point to review both computer and paper files at least twice each year deleting and discarding what is no longer needed. Make it a habit to file as little as possible, using the motto, *when in doubt, throw it out.* Research by *Stanford University* shows that we never look twice at 87 percent of the documents we file. (Source: Cole, Kris. *Make Time,* Australia: Prentice-Hall, 2001) If you toss one piece of paper every day, in only one year you'll have 365 fewer pieces of paper to clutter your office files.

Record the throw-out date on all paperwork before filing it to make purging easier. Whenever you have to retrieve something, spend a few minutes tossing out paperwork bearing expired dates.

Don't go beyond 80 percent of the capacity of the file drawer. Jamming too much stuff makes both filing and retrieval difficult. Use manila folders inside hanging folders. Thin the files on a regular basis and if you need another filing cabinet, get one. Don't stuff too many papers into hanging folders or they'll block the headings. Instead, use box bottom folders when files become thick. Start your files with only a few categories and then subdivide them as they become thick. Don't start a file for every piece of paper you receive. Keep your filing system simple. Never label a file "miscellaneous"; it becomes a tempting dumping ground and makes retrieval more difficult. Always keep the correspondence in your file folders in approximate chronological order, with the most recent items at the front.

File daily when possible. Don't let paperwork pile up. The longer you postpone filing, the more difficult it becomes and the more you will continue to delay it. You might want to set up a special time every day to do the filing and stick to it. Use 3-ring binders for filing monthly statements, reports, minutes of meetings and other documents received on a continuing basis. As you add the latest copy, toss out the oldest one to maintain them all in one binder. Use a clipped logo, masthead, cartoon, or other graphic on the spine for easy identification. Change the color of the file folders or the tabs each year. Keep current years more accessible. When archiving old files, include the throw-out date on the outside of the carton. Some files can be tossed after one year, others may have to be retained for seven or more years.

File according to where you would look for something as opposed to where it should go according to topic. The name of the game is quick retrieval. Be careful if others have to access the same records. To speed up the retrieval process, consider using the *Paper Tiger* software mentioned earlier. To control missing files, books, CDs or DVDs, you might require people to sign a "take out" sheet indicating the title of the item being borrowed, and the date borrowed.

Before tossing paperwork into a file basket, jot on it the name or the number of the file where it belongs while the topic is fresh in your mind. Otherwise you might end up re- reading it. Paste newspaper clippings onto 8½ x 11 paper to facilitate filing. Consider photocopying them first for permanence. Colored tabs that match the color of the hanging folder are pretty; but clear tabs make the titles easier to read.

The more frequently your files need to be accessed, the more accessible they should be. Everything doesn't have to be stashed out of sight. Keep files referred to daily in step files on your desk. Those accessed weekly can be on top of your credenza behind you. Monthly referrals can be in desk drawers or in file cabinets out of sight, but within reach. Less frequently accessed files can be in filing cabinets against the wall. File on-going, top-priority projects vertically in a step-file on your desk or credenza where you can access them easily.

Organization in the home

It's great to be organized in your office, but don't neglect your home. Time is wasted searching for invoices, telephone numbers, repair contract numbers, report cards and coupons. Take a few hours and develop a home filing system. Buy a cardboard filing box or use a filing cabinet. Label hanging folders with main categories such as *House, School, Legal*, etc. Then place manila folders into each hanging folder for the sub-categories. For example, *House* might be broken down into *Repairs, Mortgage* and *Insurance, Furniture* and *Fixtures*, etc. These files must be thinned out regularly. Paid invoices normally aren't required after one year. Don't keep invoices, letters, etc., simply because they bear a telephone number you might need someday. Transfer needed information into a permanent binder file.

This binder file or *Personal Organizer* binder consists of a 3-ring binder with dividers marked *Telephone Numbers, Emergency Numbers, Take-out Foods, Credit Cards,* etc. - everything you need on a day to day basis. When you buy a new appliance, furniture or garden equipment, record the relevant information under Repairs; that's probably why you'll need it someday. Record the name of the item, date and where purchased, address and phone number of supplier, warranty or repair contract number in this *Repair* section of the binder. If something breaks down that was not recorded by you (perhaps it came with the house) record the information once it becomes available - which is usually at the time it breaks down. It's hard to predict that roof shingles will fly off one day, but when they do, and you've tracked down a company that repairs roofs, record that information in the binder.

Record other numbers under the appropriate section. The credit card section should hold all your credit card numbers and where to call in case of loss. The simplest way is to lay all your credit cards on a photocopier and copy one side, then the other side, of about 12 cards at a time. Write the telephone number of the company beneath each card. Three-hole punch the sheets and place them in your binder.

Other sections which can be added to your binder include babysitter instructions, household hints, recipes and special dates (birthdays, anniversaries, and Christmas card mailing list).

It takes only minutes to record a number or file a piece of paper, but saves hours of searching and frustration later. Many of us waste time on the same things over and over again. How many times have you searched for your car keys before leaving for work, or for a pencil when you were on the telephone, or for your favorite tie or earrings when getting dressed?

This could happen once, but it should never happen the second time. Take a minute to establish fixed spots where you will keep those frequently used items - and take a few seconds to replace them after each use. Build a habit of returning the keys to the holder on the kitchen wall each time you walk into the house. And always return your earrings to the jewel box. Always hang your tie on the tie rack. Always return the pen to the holder attached to the telephone. It will be an effort at first, but soon it will become a habit like setting the alarm or brushing your teeth.

And it will save time, tempers and aggravation.

CHAPTER 7

WORK SMARTER, NOT HARDER

Do you find yourself taking work home in the evenings and on weekends from your day job? Are you under constant pressure, jumping from one task to another? Do you find yourself too involved in doing things to spend enough time on planning for greater profits?

It could be that you are not taking full advantage of one of the most important management tools - delegation. When you delegate, you are working smarter, not harder. Delegation extends results from what you can do to what you can control. It frees time for more important tasks, allows you to plan more effectively, and helps relieve the pressure of too many responsibilities, too many deadlines and too little time.

We have a lot of reasons for not delegating. We don't have time to train our team or our virtual assistant. They can't do it as well or as quickly as we can. We're afraid they might goof. But in many cases, these reasons are simply excuses. Sure it will take time to train them. However, every hour invested now will bring you hundreds of free hours in the future. It's unlikely our team or virtual assistant can do as good a job as we can. But how about when we started? We weren't always as good at our role as we are now. Be willing to accept less at first. As they become more experienced, they will improve. Sure they'll goof. Everyone makes mistakes. But that's the price we have to pay in order to free up our time, develop our team members and expand our business.

What tasks should we delegate? A good starting place is to list all the tasks we do on a recurring basis. No matter how small. They all take time. Then look for those tasks that take the biggest chunks of time. If they require little training, great. But if you must train, schedule time to do it. Perhaps a half hour each day or two hours each week. Set the time aside and stick to a regular schedule. Time you spend now will pay big dividends later.

Also, look at those jobs that don't take much time, but are repeated frequently. They usually require little training, and all those ten-minute increments add up in the course of a month or a year. You won't want to delegate critical tasks that can interrupt the flow of your business growth. Nor tasks that involve confidential information. But there are probably many tasks that someone else on your team could do for you, and would love to.

Assuming you are a team leader, a leader gets things done through other people. A leader plans, organizes, directs, trains and motivates. But a leader does not get bogged down with tasks that someone else can do, and that can help develop skills in others.

Principles of delegation

Improper delegation, however, is worse than no delegation at all. It not only creates a greater demand on your own time, but messes up your team's time as well. Be careful what you delegate, how you delegate, and to whom you delegate. Here are a few ground rules for effective delegation.

1. Don't delegate what you can eliminate. If it's not important enough for you to do personally, it's probably not important enough for your people to do either. Respect their time and their ability. Don't waste it on non-productive or unprofitable trivia. Your success can be multiplied a thousand times if you concentrate on the high-return jobs, and encourage your team members to do likewise - don't spoil it by using your people as a dumping ground for non-productive tasks.

2. Delegate the things you don't want to delegate. We tend to hang on to the things we like doing, even when they interfere with more important tasks, and even though our team members could probably do them just as well, or even better. Share the interesting tasks with your team members. One of the most important advantages of effective delegation is the fact that it enriches your team members' skills. Don't limit your delegation to the boring, repetitive tasks -look for the interesting ones as well.

3. Delegate - don't abdicate. Dumping jobs onto your team members and then disappearing is not delegation - it's business suicide. Delegation must be planned. Consult with your team members first; select people you think are capable of doing the task and would like to do the task. Train them. Delegate gradually, insist on feedback, and then leave them alone.

4. Delegate the objective, not the procedure. One of the bonuses you receive from effective delegation is the fact that in many cases the job is done better in the hands of someone else. Don't resent it, encourage it. Delegate the whole task for specific results de-emphasizing the actual procedure. Your team member, under less pressure, less harried, and with a fresh viewpoint, will likely improve upon the method you've been using. Review results, not the manner in which he or she arrived at them!

5. Don't always delegate to the most capable team members. Delegation is one of the most effective methods of developing your people. Don't continually delegate to the most capable ones, or they'll get stronger, while the weak ones get weaker. Take the extra effort to spread delegation across the board, and develop a strong team with no weak links.

6. Trust your team members. Be sure to delegate the authority, as well as the responsibility. Don't continually look over their shoulders, interfere with their methods, or jump on them when they make mistakes. Be prepared to trade short-term errors for long-term results. Maintain control without stifling initiative.

Henry Ford is claimed to have said, "If anyone is indispensable, fire him." A little extreme perhaps; but it does get the message across that team leaders who do not delegate actually impede the team's progress. If you hog all the information to yourself and refuse to delegate, quite possibly you can't be replaced. But you can't be promoted either, meaning your business will become stifled!

Rarely can a business afford to risk the life of a team by maintaining blockages. Sooner or later they must resort to surgery. One of the goals of every team leader should be to train someone else to replace him or her in certain tasks. Failure to do this blocks the possibility of promotion at all levels in the organization, and stifles initiative. Do you have training of others, and systematic delegation as one of the performance targets for team leaders in your organization? If not, consider it.

Ask your upline to delegate

Delegation is not only a great time saver; it is a people-developer. Nothing develops decision making ability and makes you more promotable than taking on greater responsibilities along with the ability to carry them out. But you cannot always assume your upline leader will delegate to you. If your upline fails to delegate, take the initiative and explain that you are ready for more responsibility. Make suggestions as to the tasks you feel you will be capable of handling if provided with adequate training. In fact there may be tasks you are capable of handling now, without any training.

Before you approach your upline leader, make sure you have done your "homework". First of all, do you have a list of personal goals? This is vital, since you will want to take on those responsibilities which will contribute to the attainment of these goals. For instance, you shouldn't take on technical jobs if your goal is to become a senior level leader. Or you shouldn't assume responsibilities that would necessitate evening involvement if it would conflict with an evening obligation or committed family time. The tasks you assume should be compatible with your goals and your availability.

Next, take a look at your present responsibilities to ensure that you don't take on more tasks than you can handle effectively. Are there some low pay-off activities that you can eliminate? Can some tasks be transferred to someone else? It would be a good idea to jot down all the activities you perform on a regular basis, along with the approximate time spent on them. Question everything you do. Your time is too valuable to be wasted on trivial items or items that will not get you to your goals. Don't become an "activity packrat" taking on more than you can effectively handle.

When you assume new tasks, don't hesitate to suggest alternative ways of doing them. In order to do this, however, you must know the purpose of the task - what is it that you are trying to accomplish? When assigning tasks, the upline leader may explain the procedure, but not the results expected. Make sure you understand the reason the task is being performed.

Don't try to turn the world upside down all at once. Too many suggested changes too soon may threaten the upline leader and cause resistance. After all, he or she may not like the inference that many of the tasks could have been performed better using other methods. It might be a good idea to follow the traditional procedure until you're sure of what you're doing. Then introduce the suggested changes gradually.

Be sure to clarify the type and frequency of feedback expected and the limit of your authority to make changes. Don't assume anything. One of the main reasons for not delegating is the lack of time for proper communications and training - so chances are the upline leader will not spend enough time during the delegation process. It's up to you to make sure you have all the information necessary.

When problems arise, think about it before rushing to the upline leader for advice. What would you do if you were the upline leader responsible for this task? Then go to the upline leader with suggested solutions instead of leaving all the decision-making to them. Your initial performance will determine the amount of authority that you are eventually given. Also, make sure you complete the tasks. Half-finished assignments are rarely appreciated. After all, that's why you got the task - to relieve pressure from the upline leader's schedule.

If you want to develop yourself and your business skills, you may have to take the initiative. By doing so, you are helping the team as well. If you find yourself with an upline leader who refuses to delegate regardless, you have a decision to make. Either be content working alongside them, or work with another upline leader that you also respect and can learn from.

Search for smarter ways

Working smarter involves more than delegation. It involves continually looking for better ways to do things. You may be performing a task that is no longer necessary or following a procedure that could be simplified. To make sure you are not using time unnecessarily, use the news reporters' standard questions: who, what, why, when, where and how.

1) Ask why it is being done, and you may be able to eliminate it.
2) Ask where it is being done, and you may find a better place to do it.
3) Ask when and you may be able to schedule it at a different, more convenient time.
4) Ask who and you will find the best person to do that particular job.
5) Ask what and you may discover you've been working on the wrong problem.
6) Ask how and you may find a better way to do it, including having it contracted out.

When you examine how you do things you may be able to incorporate many shortcuts. Much time is wasted by meetings, travel, and non-productive telephone calls. Look at these areas to see what efficiencies could be made.

Meetings

Many people actually dread meetings. After all, they have a reputation for being time wasting, boring, and non-productive. Yet meetings provide an excellent way of improving productivity. Don't shy away from meetings. Instead, prepare well in advance to get the most out of each meeting you attend or conduct. Be skilled in supporting your team members at meetings by meeting their guests, edifying them to their guests and their own team members, and provide them with additional tips during break time which they can apply to their business.

When conducting meetings as a leader, be skilled in conducting an informative, fun and fast-paced meeting so that all who are in attendance will walk away feeling like their time was well invested, and their lives enhanced. Below are meeting principles that will bring about such results.

1. **Set measurable objectives.** Set objectives in such a way that you can measure the results at a later date. Do you want people to understand certain procedures, increase sales, reduce costs, solve a problem? Include the objectives on the agenda and on a flip chart or blackboard in the meeting room. If your meeting starts to drift in a direction that will not help to reach your objective, pull it back on course.

2. **Plan your meeting.** Develop a detailed outline or agenda and send it out to all program participants well in advance. Detail the starting time, ending time, time allocated to each topic area, and the individuals responsible for each part of the agenda, as well as the meeting set up and logistics. Make it clear that any handouts should be ready to go before the meeting, and people assigned to distribute them. When drawing up the agenda, make sure the most important items appear first.

3. **Select the meeting place carefully.** It should take place away in a central location that team members can easily get to by car, or transit. The meeting cost for attendees needs to be considered as a major factor because business builders who are just getting started may see the cost of parking and admission as a deterrent from attending, and yet you want to ensure your costs are covered. The room needs to be well ventilated, not too warm, and with enough space to allow the participants to stretch out. Use visual aids of some kind - flipcharts, blackboard, or overhead projector - to increase retention. Have upbeat music playing as attendees arrive and at break times. This creates the positive energy required for attendees to be receptive to what information you are delivering.

4. **Stick to your schedule.** Start the meeting on time, regardless. If you're the only one there on time, talk to yourself until the others arrive! Don't recap with every late arrival. Delaying the meeting simply encourages lateness. At the start, explain what will be covered and why. Re-state the objectives. Keep to the agenda and don't allow participants to take off on tangents.

5. **Maintain control.** Guard against one or two people monopolizing the meeting. Encourage

everyone to participate when it is open discussion time and watch for those non-verbal signals that indicate someone doesn't understand, objects, or wishes to speak. Listen more than you talk during the open mic time. One study revealed that the average meeting leader takes 60% of the conference time to speak themselves. If it's one way communication you want, forget about a meeting and send a memo instead.

6. **Summarize meeting objectives at the end.** The meeting is over when you have accomplished your objectives, so don't let it drag on, but also make sure the attendees are going home with what you intended for them. Make sure the training and information delivered are clear, and send attendees home with a clear call to action so the objectives are applied.

There are several good books available which discuss meeting management at length, including *Manage Your Meetings* by Harold Taylor. It's a good investment of time to study the subject further.

Travel time

There are many ways you could save time while traveling as well. If a person works 8 hours per day, and drives 10,000 miles in a year at 40 mph, he or she spends over 31 days traveling. If you have 10 employees traveling the same 10,000 miles, you are paying the equivalent of another employee just to cover the travel time.

Unfortunately, we can't simply beam ourselves to our destination in Star Trek fashion. But what we can do is more effectively utilize our own travel time and encourage our employees to do likewise. Once your route has been designed to minimize traveling time, there are still several ways of productively utilizing the time still spent behind the wheel.

Professional development. There are excellent audio recordings available - everything from condensations of best-selling books to motivational and sales training CDs. This is far more productive than listening to the same news over and over again on the radio. And it can reap benefits in terms of professional development.

Dictation. Letters, reports, sales quotas, follow-up lists, ideas can all be dictated into a small digital recorder while parked, or into your iPhone which provides such features. This will reduce the time normally spent on paperwork later. It also prevents you from forgetting those creative ideas that seem to pop up out of nowhere.

Planning. Driving time can be utilized for planning the day, rehearsing a presentation, solving a problem or reviewing and evaluating the day's activities. To be effective, however, you must be able to discipline yourself. Your mind has a tendency to wander away and engage in a little extracurricular daydreaming. Your priority is your driving.

Relaxation. You mustn't lose sight of the fact that on occasion you should do nothing except relax and listen to music. It clears the cobwebs after a particularly hectic morning. A relaxation break is productive when it revitalizes you for the tasks ahead.

Quiet hour. During a heavy traffic hold-up, or when a long drive has made you particularly weary, you should consider pulling off the road and setting up office for an hour. In fact it might be a good idea to make it a habit every day - perhaps while you're still in a client's parking lot. Your car should be equipped with everything you need to schedule your next day's clients, summarize reports and statistics, and update your log book. This *quiet hour* in the car assures you of interruption-free time away from the hustle and bustle of the office. Unencumbered with telephone interruptions and visitors, your paperwork can be dispensed with quickly.

Here are a few more hints on saving time while on the road:

1. Plan your travel route in advance. Make sure your latest sales calls are closest to your home or office. You will waste less time sitting in rush hour traffic.

2. Use a checklist to ensure that you have everything you need for the trip, including addresses and phone numbers, change for parking meters, your planner and materials to review with the clients. Think the trip through chronologically as you make the list so you won't forget anything.

3. Be sure to take reading material with you for those inevitable waits in reception rooms.

4. Keep records on all your sales calls. List what went right, what went wrong, follow- ups required, and problems to be solved. Do it immediately following the call. Don't leave it until you get back to the office. Relying on your memory can be a major time waster.

5. If you have to travel a considerable distance to make one sales call, determine what other prospects you can visit while in the area. You'll reduce the travel time per call.

A McGraw-Hill survey revealed that the average salesperson only spends 39% of his or her time in front of prospects, while traveling and waiting time takes up 32%. Just think what the results would be if face to face selling time could be increased to 50%.

This could be easily accomplished if travel and waiting time were utilized to record reminders and reports, dispense with paperwork, plan, summarize sales calls, listen to audio CDs, and anything else that normally fills the 29% of a salesperson's job still remaining.

Time is the ultimate money. Everyone has the same amount; no more, no less. How effective we are depends on how we utilize it.

The telephone

Most people see the telephone as a major time waster, but when used properly, it can slice up to an hour from your day.

For example, it can eliminate some time-consuming appointments you might tend to make. When someone asks for an appointment to see you, find out what he or she wants. Chances are you'll be able to settle it right there on the phone.

This could also apply to customers with a problem. Find out the details on the phone. Don't go running to put out fires until you know all the facts. With a little guidance from you, the customer may be able to solve his or her own problem. Keep in mind that the customer's objective is not to see you in person, but to get out of trouble quickly.

The phone can also be used to reduce the number of emails and memos. Many emails you receive are simply asking a question or requesting information. Resist the urge to write back. Pick up the phone and give your answer verbally. It's usually faster, less expensive, and impresses the sender. And with voice mail you don't even have to talk to the person. If you need written confirmation, write, but don't write if you don't have to.

The telephone can also be used to replace meetings. Conference calls not only save the time of participants, but eliminate any travel costs.

If you want the telephone to work for you, you must take advantage of as many time-saving strategies as possible. Here are more suggestions:

1. Group the callbacks. Get in the habit of accumulating your messages and returning the calls in a group. Just before noon is a good time, since conversations tend to be briefer when they threaten to interfere with lunch. About 4:30 p.m. is a good time to return the afternoon calls.

2. Record the best time of the day or week to get through to the people you phone on a regular basis. Include this information in your telephone directory.

3. Always give your name when asking to speak to someone. Don't make the receptionist wheedle it out of you.

4. Ask as few questions as possible. It will keep the conversation shorter. Be polite, but brief. Discuss the business first and socialize later.

5. If you have an assistant, have the calls intercepted and handled (where possible) by that person when you are busy with important work. Or engage the voice mail.

6. If the person you're calling is busy, don't get in the habit of holding unless you have a lot of routine work you can do while you wait. Leave a voice mail message instead.

7. If the person you're calling is not there, try to get the information you need from someone else rather than leave a message to call back.

8. Take notes on all calls; they will likely result in follow-ups, and making mental notes is not time-effective.

9. Arrange your callbacks in order of importance, in case you're interrupted before you finish.

Remember to question everything you do. Always search for easier and faster ways of doing things. Work smarter, not harder.

CHAPTER 8

AVOID THE TYRANNY OF THE URGENT

Don't let the urgent things crowd out the important. Since many important items don't have to be done right away, managers tend to delay them in favor of those urgent, yet unimportant, tasks that demand their attention.

As a result, those important items eventually become urgent as well. And you're continually faced with a mixture of important and unimportant items, all urgent. You attempt to respond to them all, procrastinating on any additional important items that arise. Unfortunately, the number of urgent tasks exceeds your capacity to carry them out. You're under constant pressure. Some important tasks fall through the cracks, decreasing your effectiveness and increasing your anxiety. You may end up with an ulcer, nervous breakdown, heart attack or stroke.

Cut off this vicious circle at its source. Don't automatically respond to the urgent. Differentiate between the important and the unimportant. Important tasks are those which contribute to the attainment of your personal or organizational goals. They have intrinsic value. Spend time on these important tasks *before* they become urgent.

There's nothing threatening about important tasks. They're challenging. Rewarding. They help develop your ability and skills. And they have a major impact on organizational goals. But when they're allowed to become urgent, they become a threat... something to be dispensed with quickly. As a result they are seldom performed as effectively as they could have been.

In order to determine which tasks are important and which ones are unimportant, you must stop and take inventory. The busier you get, the more you need this time of inventory, but the less chance you have of taking it. You become like the boy lost in the woods who doubles his speed to make up for a lack of direction. I know you haven't got time to stop. But stop anyway. Let a few urgent tasks go undone. That's the short-term price you have to pay for long-term results.

Focus on your goals

Once you've stopped and collected your thoughts, write out your long-range and short- range goals. A goal in your head is a dream. But a goal on paper is an objective. Objectives are specific. Measurable. Attainable. They allow you to formulate a plan of action to achieve them. And they reveal whether those urgent tasks hanging over your head are really important or not. If they will not help you reach your goals, ignore them. If you feel they are still important for other reasons, delegate them. But don't waste your time on them.

Instead, devote your time to those really important tasks which will provide the results you are looking for. Do the urgent ones first. But not before scheduling the others. For the trick is to do all the important tasks *before* they become urgent. Sure, there'll be the odd vitally-important task that suddenly pops out of nowhere. But most of the important tasks make themselves known in advance. You should schedule blocks of time in your planning calendar to do them. "To do" lists encourage the tyranny of the urgent. The first jobs you think of are those that are urgent and they're the first to be worked on. So if you have enough urgent tasks you may never get around to those important, non- urgent tasks that relate to your goals. So be sure to use your time planner to schedule those important tasks in your planner. Don't bury them on a "to do" list. Once you commit these blocks of time to valuable, meaningful activities, they are unavailable to other people. Other meetings and appointments will have to be scheduled around them.

Question these other activities. Can they be eliminated? Or simplified? Can they be delegated to someone else? Why do you have to attend that meeting? Can you attend only part of it? Or send someone in your place? Any activity that will not bring you closer to your personal or company goals should be suspect. Time is your most valuable resource. It is life itself. So give it up grudgingly. Don't see visitors unless they have an appointment. Try to settle matters on the telephone, eliminating the necessity of a personal appointment.

Unrealistic deadlines also promote urgency. It's possible that you work harder and faster under the pressure of unrealistic deadlines, but it's doubtful that you work better. Excellence does not come from tired, harried people. Mediocrity does. You would hate to have your plane piloted by someone who had been flying steadily for 12 hours. And you probably wouldn't feel too comfortable in a taxi if the driver had been driving all night. It's a fact that tired workers cause accidents. For the same reason, most skiing mishaps take place during that "one last run".

Don't talk yourself into believing that working steadily with your nose to the grindstone will lead to success. It will only lead to a flat nose. Work smarter, not harder. Concentrate on the goals you set for yourself. Every day do something to bring yourself closer to them. But recognize that you will have to ignore some of those unimportant, but urgent, activities that produce minimal results. You can't do everything and still keep your life in balance.

To prevent yourself from filling your planning calendar with business-related activities, schedule blocks of leisure time. Schedule time for outings with the children, a movie with your spouse, a tennis game or shopping trip. Schedule them in ink, not pencil; make them definite, not tentative. Most people schedule them with the idea that they will go through with it "if something more important doesn't come up". And the "something more important" is usually job-related, and usually involves value in terms of dollars and cents.

Recognize that leisure time has value, too. Not in terms of measurable "dollars and cents", but in terms of long-term effectiveness; in terms of family accord and happiness; in terms of physical health and mental alertness. And in terms of success.

Keep your life in perspective

Marilyn Machlowitz, in her book, *Workaholics,* quotes a case study recorded by Robert Coles, a Harvard psychiatrist. It involves Helen, aged 10, whose words contain a lesson for any of us who unthinkingly devote most of our time and energies to our jobs:

> *"There's only one reason I like to go to our country home - because Daddy is there. All week we don't see much of him. Sometimes I'm lucky if I see him for five minutes in the morning before I go to school... and a lot of times he doesn't get home before we go to bed. I miss him. So does my brother, Geoff. He says he wishes Daddy would lose his job, then we'd have him here at home. Geoff says he even prays that Daddy will lose his job."*

Keep your job - and your life - in perspective. With so much emphasis on success and achievement it sometimes becomes difficult to relax and enjoy life. Don't set your sights too high. Do the best you can, but don't kill yourself. Job burnout is a result of too much stress, and most jobs are stressful enough without adding your own unrealistic goals and expectations.

Set realistic goals. And realize that you can't do everything. Work on priorities - the 20 percent of activities which will bring you 80 percent of the results.

And always have some way of working off mental and emotional stress. Engage in a regular exercise program. Have interests other than your job. Make it a habit to talk over your problems with a close friend.

Above all, remember that what you are is more important than what you do.

Don't get trapped in the rapid stream of life with its rushing flood of activities. We live in a dangerous world where nine tenths of the accidents on streets and in homes are caused by careless rushing. We accelerate through life attempting to accomplish too many things in too little time. We dash from one job to the next, one appointment to the next, bent on beating unrealistic deadlines.

As a result, we suffer stress, hypertension, stomach disorders, headaches, insomnia. Many of us are rewarded with heart attacks, bleeding ulcers, nervous breakdowns. We are filled with anxiety, worry, despair, frustration and even fear. We are gradually committing suicide.

And for what? Are we racing toward that elusive goal called success? Are we trying to keep pace with the professional sprinters of the world? Is everyone our competitor? Are we trying to prove something? Impress someone? Gain riches?

Step off the race track for a minute. Take time from your busiest day to reflect on what you are doing and where you are headed. As you speed ahead, are you leaving neglected families, injured friends and heart-broken loved ones in your wake? Are you really accomplishing the goal you thought you were aiming at? Or has the race itself obscured the goal? Are you so engrossed in the race that you have lost sight of the finish line?

Sometimes, we get caught up in the current of those around us. Move to a large city and soon you are whisked along at the pace of the city dwellers. Join a large corporation, and you soon move at the pace of the organization man. Start your own business and you accelerate to the speed of an entrepreneur. Are we really individuals? Are we really in control of our own lives?

We can be. But only if we make a conscious effort to choose our own track. Move at our own speed toward the finish line. The things which are meaningful to others may not be meaningful to us. Life is a beautiful track; it consists of more than a finish line. There is scenery. And fun. And laughter. And love. There are the sounds of children. The smell of flowers. The touch of loved ones.

Life need not be a race. It could be a stroll. If you love life, don't speed past it so quickly. Slow down. Pause a while. You can't stop completely. But you can drift along in a lower gear, enjoying all that it has to offer. You don't have to be caught up in the tyranny of the urgent just because everyone else seems to be.

The hurry and wait society

Why do we always speed up when approaching an orange light so we can get to the next one just as it turns red? Or rush to the supermarket or bank and then wait in line for twenty minutes? Or race downtown to arrive fifteen minutes early for an appointment?

We are caught in a hurry and wait society. Rush here. Rush there. And wait, wait, wait. It's symptomatic of a lack of planning. We don't fill our gas tank if it's only three quarters empty, even if there's no lineup at the gas pumps. Instead we wait until the gauge indicates "empty" and we take a ten block detour to find a service station and wait behind three other cars. We don't telephone ahead to make an appointment and as a result end up waiting in a lobby for twenty minutes. We don't ask for detailed directions and waste time searching for an address. We don't make advance reservations at a restaurant and end up waiting fifteen minutes for a table. Planning saves time, reduces the need to hurry and eliminates a lot of waiting.

But sometimes even planning doesn't help. We're in an age of line-ups. We wait in line at subways and airports, restaurants, stores, banks and government offices. We're kept waiting in reception rooms, at meetings, in business offices and in parking lots and on highways. The combination of our internal "let's get moving" plea and the external "you'll have to wait" response produces frustration, anxiety and stress. And if it's greater than our ability to cope, we end up with yet another frustrating wait; in a doctor's reception room or a hospital emergency ward.

You can't keep your mind in gear while you have the brake on. Getting upset over line-ups won't gain time, only ulcers. To survive we must remain calm and make use of this idle time. Always bring reading material with you- and a yellow highlighter to mark significant areas for later reference. If you don't feel self-conscious, use a digital recorder to dictate memos or ideas. Or plan your week, review your goals, or perform mathematical tasks on your PDA calculator or make your calls using a cell phone. If you're busy at something productive, you won't be as conscious of that lineup. Time will seem to pass more quickly. And you'll be making effective use of your time.

It's not the speed at which you race through life that counts; it's what you get accomplished en route. And you are able to accomplish much more if you coast at a slower speed.

Don't be a "rushaholic"

Meyer Friedman, co-author of *Type A Behavior and Your Heart,* claimed in an article in "Reader's Digest" that whenever a man struggles incessantly to accomplish too many things in too little time, and struggles too competitively with other individuals, this struggle markedly accentuates the course of coronary heart disease. Although people wouldn't dare race the engines of their cars day after day, and expect it to endure, they race their own engines at a frightfully increasing pace - and leave survivors who are shocked at their abrupt breakdown.

Dr. Friedman suggests that we begin to value friendship again. And that the friends we seek must be people who don't necessarily admire us as much as they love us. We should reevaluate our use of time, making fewer appointments and ceasing to harass ourselves. He suggests we repeatedly ask ourselves the question, "What difference will it truly make in five years if the departure of my plane is delayed?"

We seem to be so afraid of killing time, that we are letting time kill *us.* Don't let busyness, line-ups, or the tyranny of the urgent rob you of a happy, healthy, and time- filled life.

John Edmond Haggai, in his book, *How to Win Over Worry* maintains that we should have periodic breaks in our activities if we want to work under pressure without working under tension. Haggai claims that a change in activity could constitute a rest. It is only by this procedure that our heart continues to work for eighty years or so. It pumps enough blood through our body every twenty-four hours to fill a railway tanker. Every day it exerts as much effort as it would take to shovel twenty tons of gravel onto a platform as high as our waist. The reason it can do this incredible amount of work is because when it is beating moderately it works only nine hours out of twenty-four. So don't think periodic rest periods are a waste of time.

Our bodies aren't made for "round the clock" use. Analyze your workday and you'll realize that 80 percent of your productive work gets done in 20 percent of the time. The rest of the time we coast, dawdle, shuffle papers, waste time. Recharge your batteries during the day and you will increase that time of high productivity. Go for a walk. Then resume work refreshed.

Remember that life isn't a work-a-thon. Plan those vacations throughout the year and stick to your plan. Don't let it be said that you have a better preventative maintenance program for your office and plant equipment than you have for your own body. Take time to relax.

Antonia Van Der Meer, writing in McCall's magazine, was quoted by *Communications Briefing* as offering the following tips on coping with what he referred to as "Rushaholism":

Are you a "rushaholic"? Do you over-schedule? Walk and talk too fast? Interrupt others so you can get things done quickly?

Consider these tips:

(1) Don't do more than one thing at a time.

(2) Say "no" more often.

(3) View your life as a puzzle with too many pieces. Throw some out.

(4) Schedule quiet time for yourself in your appointment book.

(5) Take a one-minute vacation in your mind. Think of a place where you felt relaxed.

(6) Talk and eat more slowly. Drive in the slow lane once in a while.

(7) Leave your watch at home.

(8) Don't add unless you subtract. Volunteer to do something only after you give up another task.

A little pressure is a good thing

Some activities are really urgent - we're put under pressure to look after them right away - even though they're not that important. That's bad. Some activities are important inasmuch as they offer opportunities - either for improved quality, reduced costs, increased sales, etc. - but nobody is really pushing for them (they may not even be *aware* of them) and so there is *no* pressure. That's also bad.

A little pressure moves a project or task to completion. It forces people to meet deadlines. It overcomes inertia, procrastination, and the inclination to waste time or get side-tracked. A little pressure produces results. It's also stimulating. It makes you feel alive. Active. Productive.

Unfortunately, the pressure is usually applied for those routine, low-value activities that everyone is aware should be done at specific times. But those same activities rarely contribute to organizational goals. They're usually of a "housekeeping" nature as opposed to creative, profit-generating activities. These latter ideas usually lie dormant within us, waiting for the moment that we have time to express them and work on them. But that time never comes. Because we are constantly under pressure to complete those mundane, low-value tasks.

A little pressure is a good thing, but make sure you apply it at the right time, and on the right activities. Don't place the emphasis on those routine tasks. Eliminate some of them. Delegate others. Then schedule specific times to work on those ideas that seem to hang at the back of your mind. Those ideas that could increase productivity and profits. Set deadlines for yourself. Pressure is a lot easier to take when it involves creative, challenging tasks that produce a sense of achievement.

Time hassles

Richard Lazarus, writing in an issue of *Psychology Today*, reported that those minor, daily events such as losing a wallet, or getting caught in a traffic jam can be more harmful than those infrequent, major events such as divorce, retirement or being fired.

Those minor, daily events have a greater effect on our moods and our health. These effects vary according to their frequency, intensity and our reaction to them. When under pressure, those petty problems can have a much greater effect than if they had occurred at less anxious times. Stress is not caused by the event itself, but by our reaction to it.

The top three hassles revealed in a survey were misplacing or losing things, physical appearance, and too many things to do. Time management will do nothing to improve physical appearance, but it can certainly help out with the other two. Organizing yourself and your environment should alleviate the first problem, and getting rid of the trivia in your life and concentrating on priorities should relieve the other hassle.

Regardless of how effectively we manage our time, there will always be some hassles in our lives. Lazarus suggests that uplifts may serve as emotional buffers against disorders brought on by hassles. Uplifts include such activities as enjoying yourself with good friends, spending time with the family, eating out and getting enough sleep. And don't forget the importance of your *reaction* to hassles. If you can shrug them off or even laugh at them, without letting them get you all tense and upset, you've got them licked.

Personality and stress

The effect that life crises, stressful events, and working environments actually do have on you is dependent to a great extent upon your individual personality - the other factor which is believed to be a major factor in heart disease. Rosenman and Friedman found that people exhibiting "Type A" behavior are over twice as prone to heart attacks, five times more prone to a second attack and have had fatal heart attacks twice as frequently.

The Type A personality is characterized by intensive drive and aggressiveness. He/she is ambitious, competitive, feels a constant pressure to get things done and often races the clock. He/she is restless, hates to be idle and can't stand lineups. He/she is impatient, a hard worker, speaks, eats and moves quickly, and schedules more and more in less and less time.

In contrast, the Type B individuals are relatively free of any sense of time urgency, pressing conflicts or impatience. They are equally or more effective, working smarter, not harder. They also have significantly less risk of coronary disease.

Rosenman claims that "in the absence of Type A behavior pattern, coronary heart disease almost never occurs before seventy years of age, regardless of the fatty foods eaten, the cigarettes smoked, or the lack of exercise. But when this behavioral pattern is present, coronary heart disease can easily erupt in one's thirties or forties."

This is quite a claim, and whether it is accepted without question or not, it does emphasize the importance of how we *react* to the stressful environment and constant crises with which most managers are faced.

If you try to do everything yourself, are always running out of time, and have an unrealistic sense of time urgency, you may possess a "Type A" personality style. "Type A" managers are generally easily irritated, insecure, aggressive and competitive- and stand a greater risk of having a heart attack.

Dr. Meyer Friedman, co-author of the best seller, *Type A Behavior and Your Heart*, has shown that Type A counseling *does* work. In a three-year experiment involving 862 people who had one or more heart attacks, doctors discovered that those receiving Type A counseling had fewer recurring heart attacks.

The advice given: walk, talk and eat more slowly, play games to lose, write down things that spark anger, smile at others and laugh at yourself, do one thing at a time, admit to being wrong, and stop interrupting. The participants were taught to slow down and get more done.

The *Chicago Tribune* reported that one manager receiving such counseling used to twitch, sigh, answer questions without a moment's thought, and get angry at slow drivers and long lines. Now he listens to music in the car, stops at yellow lights rather than racing through them and observes others while waiting in lineups, imagining what their lives are like.

Learn to recognize stress

Most managers recognize stress even though they may not be able to describe it easily. It normally precipitates emotional discomfort, a feeling that not all is well, helplessness, a fear of not being able to cope. It could include loss of appetite, insomnia, sweating, ulcers or other illnesses. It is brought on by what is described as the "fight or flight response" - an involuntary body response which increases our blood pressure, heart rate, rate of breathing, blood flow to the muscles and metabolism - preparing us to face some conflict or flee some danger. The body is prepared for some physical activity, but the activity never comes because most of today's situations call for behavioral adjustments, not physical activity. Consequently our body's systems are thrown out of balance.

The fight or flight response could be elicited when you are suddenly cut off by another car during your hectic drive to the office one morning. The body's responses prepare you for "fight" but instead you sit there and stew - your hands clenching the wheel, face flushed, stomach muscles tight. The appropriate response might be to jump out of the car, yank open the antagonist's door, pull him out by the scruff of the neck and smack him a good one. But although this would invariably relieve the tension, it is only appropriate from the viewpoint of our body's system and not from the viewpoint of acceptable behavior as far as society is concerned. Consequently, we remain under stress after the cause of it has disappeared.

A similar reaction could take place when confronted by dozens of little tasks all due at the same time. Urgency, combined with a predisposition to Type A behavior, can become a health threatening experience. Medical and psychological problems caused by stress have become a major health problem. One standard medical text estimates that 50% to 80% of all diseases have their origins in stress.

One of the many diseases often associated with stress is that of heart disease. It is claimed that 50% of all premature deaths among males are from coronary disease. If you are a male over 40 years old, you have a 50-50 chance of dying from a heart attack. The odds are even worse if you're a "Type A" person, which indicates the importance of your personality and how you react when subjected to a potentially stressful situation such as the careless motorist referred to earlier.

It's been said that if traditional risk factors could be controlled, such as blood pressure, smoking, cholesterol, heredity, etc. - only about 25% of all heart disease would be eliminated. The other 75%, or most of it, is a result of personality and environment.

Studies have indicated that the following attitudes protect people against stress:

Control: feeling in charge of a situation.
Commitment: committed to the task and believing in yourself.
Challenge: looking at change as a positive challenge, not a threat.

According to research conducted by Suzanne C. Kobasa, a graduate student at the *University of Chicago*, attitudes towards stressful events are much more important than the events themselves. A study of 670 male managers revealed that the high-stress low-illness group was high in all three attitudes, as measured by personality tests. A second study, which followed 259 executives over a two-year period, gave the same results. People whose attitudes were high in control, commitment, and challenge, were healthier at the start and remained healthier than their peers.

Haste makes waste

"Haste makes waste" is not a useless bromide. It's a fact. People who don't have time to do something right always seem to find the time to do it over again. It's always better to negotiate a later deadline than to rush something, but even if you *must work* under stress, don't panic. Take a minute of the precious time available, and plan how you will do it, break up the task if possible and determine how much time you can afford to spend on each part of it, reschedule any less urgent jobs which might interfere with it, and take precautions to prevent interruptions. Then work methodically, thoughtfully. Don't work in a frenzy. If you fail to get it done, probably it was an impossibility in the first place.

In summary then, remember that it's not how many things you do, but what you accomplish that counts. Don't lose sight of your goals, and concentrate on that 20% of the activities that produce 80% of the results. Don't get caught up in the hurry-and-wait society. Maintain control of yourself. Organize your space, have a clean desk. Get in the habit of scheduling important items in your time planner and get rid of those scraps of paper with those lists of urgent items that may bear little importance. Recognize that you can't do everything. Question unrealistic deadlines. Modify your tendency toward Type A behavior by putting first things first, delegating, and letting some of the trivia fall by the wayside. Relax more. Take an occasional break, and don't let work become an obsession. Vacations should be one of the first activities you schedule into next year's planner.

Conclusion

Just as budgets in themselves don't improve spending habits, so time management seminars, books, or audio recordings, don't improve time-wasting habits. In the case of budgets, many people simply peruse them, smile or grimace, and then continue to do what they always do. Budgets simply keep score. Similarly, time management seminars, books and CDs, reveal what you are doing wrong. They pinpoint the time wasting habits, reveal methods for improving the way you are managing time, and suggest a strategy for getting more done in less time.

Unfortunately, most people make a half-hearted effort to try a few of the techniques suggested, achieve a small degree of success, and gradually revert to their original habits. Meanwhile, the seminar manuals, DVDs, action sheets, books and notes lie in disuse under their desk or in a bookcase or filing cabinet.

To change spending habits and keep costs in line, you must make permanent changes and doggedly persist in your efforts. So with time management; you must resolve to curb the flagrant spending of time. This involves effort. Persistence. Determination. Seldom does anything worthwhile come easily. Don't look upon this training unit as a one-shot deal. Look at it as only the first step in a series of steps to gain permanent control of your spending of time.

The second step should be taken immediately, before you toss the materials aside.

Schedule time in your planner to put into action a few of the better suggestions. Devote at least one hour each day thereafter to changing forms, methods, materials, and reinforcing new behaviors.

Never squeeze a seminar or other training session between two business meetings or other obligations. Schedule enough time to do something with the information you have gleaned from the session. Seminars or audio recordings cannot change behavior. But people can change their own behavior as a result of the material discussed.

But it requires that you budget sufficient time for it. And that you take action right away while the motivation to do something is strong.

So review this material, and take action in the eight key areas that will keep you organized. Set goals and priorities. Plan and schedule. Write things down. Don't procrastinate. Don't be a packrat. Store things in an orderly way. Work smarter, not harder. And avoid the tyranny of the urgent. Keep working at it until you build habits: good habits that will increase your effectiveness. Not only will you get more out of each day. You will get more out of life.

CHAPTER NINE

TAKE CHARGE OF TECHNOLOGY

About 20 years ago, I wrote a brief article praising the merits of dictating letters directly into a pocket recorder and having them transcribed by a secretary or assistant. It was a lot faster and cheaper than dictating directly to a person taking shorthand, or writing longhand and having them typed. I even quoted cost comparisons.

Times have changed. With the advent of computers, it became far less expensive and more expedient to type your own letters, use the spell check option, fax, e-mail or print directly from your computer, and file at the click of a mouse – into your electronic "Documents" file or into the clouds. And typing speed became a big factor in the efficiency game.

While visiting a computer outlet to buy a typing skills software program many years ago, I was asked whether I did a lot of typing. When I answered in the affirmative, the sales rep suggested I buy software that allows one to dictate directly to the computer. "Why learn to type," he asked, "when you can simply talk."

We've come a long way since then. The voice activated software becomes more efficient as the years go by, and the greatest time savers haven't been invented yet. We must keep up to date on these latest innovations if we are to maximize the use of our time.

Now we can scan business cards directly into a database, use PIM's the size of credit cards, talk via cell phones that can hide in the palm of your hand, and install OCR software that allows us to edit and reissue books, articles, procedures and guidelines that were written twenty years ago. We can use a computer indexing system that will allow us to instantly access anything in our files. Or we can convert our files to digital through document imaging. We can use the Internet to receive up-to-the-minute information on plane arrivals, download articles in our area of interest or talk to people on the other side of the world without spending a penny through programs like SKYPE.

Websites can save you time

The Internet must be the biggest timesaving innovation since the advent of the computer. Everyone has a favorite website or two where they can obtain information, download software or purchase products or services. It is like having a reference library, fully equipped office and a shopping mall all at your fingertips at all times. It's as portable as a laptop and available at work, home or on the road.

You could use Google or MapBlast for directions to specific locations. If you want to check an area code to identify the origin of a voice mail message before returning the call, visit http://www.bennetyee.org/ucsd-pages/area.html. You may want to print the entire list and have a permanent reference list.

If you are interested in setting goals in any area of your life with or without an accountability partner, there is a free service at http://www.stickk.com/ that might be worth a look. Information and inspiration for setting and keeping New Year's Resolutions and opportunity to share your intents and view other's commitments are available at. http://www.intent.com/. If you feel you need reminders and motivators to help you to get things done, you might try this website. Every day they email you to ask, "What'd you get done today?" Based on your replies they keep tabs for you on a calendar showing what you have accomplished. http://idonethis.com/

Can't find your cell phone? Well of course the first thing you do is call your number and listen for the ring. But what if you don't have another phone to call from? Then go to this website and enter your cell phone number and they will call it for you: www.wheresmycellphone.com.

There is a *Meeting Ticker* online that measures how much money is spent attending meetings. You enter the number of attendees and average hourly salary. The meeting start time is already recorded for you), and watch the dollars add up in real time. An interesting use of this is to use it for your tasks and see how much those emails are costing you for instance. Check it out at http://tobytripp.github.com/meeting-ticker/

Bookboon.com offers free ebooks on a variety of topics. For instance you can download Harold's book, *Time to be Productive* by going to http://bookboon.com/en/time-to-be-productive-ebook. There are plenty of others.

When recommending websites you might want to make sure they are safe first. You can do that at http://safeweb.norton.com/. Use it before you visit the ones mentioned here.

One software program that has saved us a lot of time is *Shortkeys* from www.shortkeys.com. It eliminates repetitive typing and the possibility of errors by allowing us to insert up to 3000 keystrokes of boilerplate material into a document or e-mail message with a few strokes of the keyboard.

There are so many interesting websites that you could easily lose track of the time you spend at some of the "fun" websites. If you think it may be consuming too much of your valuable time, set a time limit using http://keepmeout.com/en/ and it will block you from entering more frequently than you specify.

Just like all timesaving devices, whether they are computers, telephones, e-mail or voice mail, the Internet can become a timewaster if not used properly. Surfing the web with no particular goal in mind will lead you on an interesting but possibly unproductive journey. Maintain a list of reference websites that you can visit for specific information. When you read or hear of another website that you think might be useful, add it to your list. You will be building an invaluable resource that will save you time and effort in the future.

There is no limit to what we can or will be able to do in the future to increase our efficiency and personal productivity. The trouble is, most of us are too busy with our current projects to keep up to date with technology. There may come a time when hiring someone on a part-time or contract basis simply to keep on top of the latest innovations and determine how they could be applied to our operations might be economically feasible. Otherwise we'll be hanging up on vendors advocating the use of their latest high-tech gizmos simply because we don't have time to talk to them.

One thing's certain. Since we are still in the information age and entering the digital age of speed, we must find a way to not only cope with it, but to take advantage of it. Perhaps a worthwhile goal would be investigate the feasibility of adopting at least one timesaving, cost-reducing technological innovation in each year. There are plenty to go around.

The limits of technology

Technology can reduce the time it takes to launch a new product; but it doesn't tell us whether the new product should be launched. It may help us write a letter faster; but it doesn't tell us what do say. It can provide unlimited data, statistics and research in a matter of minutes; but it doesn't deposit it into our memory banks, sort out the material of specific use or apply the information to our particular situation. In fact, technology can actually work *against* us since it can speed us up in the wrong direction. If you are poor at decision-making, speed will only aggravate the situation. If you have the wrong goals, technology will only get you to the wrong place faster. If you are disorganized, it will simply speed up your disorganization.

Technology has been a great assist in the quest for increased productivity. But with it comes the necessity to improve our management and people skills. We must fine-tune our decision-making ability, have a clear vision of where we want to go, and set realistic, meaningful goals. Direction is more important than speed.

In some ways, our quest for increased productivity has backfired. Harvard researchers have determined that talking on cell phones while driving causes 6% of the accidents each year, killing an estimated 2600 people at an annual cost of $43 million. Multitasking, meant to *increase* efficiency, has had the opposite effect, *decreasing* efficiency as much as 50 percent. And the mass of information available on the Internet has caused what the late great Zig Ziglar called "paralysis by analysis", time loss and stress.

A U. K. study reported that 42% of respondents attributed their ill health to information overload.

Do a simple Google search on the words *information overload* and you will have enough reading material to last a lifetime. A 2000 study conducted at the *University of California*, Berkeley revealed that we produce 1.5 gigabytes of content each year. And that was over ten years ago!

The information explosion, technology and increasing demands on our time have changed the way salespeople and others must operate in order to remain effective. Time, more than ever before, is being recognized as an individual's most valuable, non-renewable asset. And time management is viewed more as an investment strategy than an efficiency tool. *The Law of Diminishing Returns*, the *Pareto Principle* and *Parkinson's Law* all take on a new importance in an age where *"Not To Do"* lists are more meaningful than *"To Do"* lists.

After conducting time management training for over thirty-five years, Harold has concluded that there should be a shift in emphasis from efficiency to effectiveness. While they are both important, purpose is more important than procedure, a healthy lifestyle is more important than a hundred time-saving tactics, and attitude is more important than solitude when it comes to increasing personal productivity. Workshop topics are now including the theory of time investments, the dangers of multitasking, building stress resistance, controlling technology and holistic time management. Time management training should also include survival skills to cope with the smaller work areas, less privacy, increased accessibility, longer working hours and increased demands that have all been precipitated by our continuing quest for increased efficiency. Self-control is more important than ever as the cost of procrastination becomes greater. Perfectionism, once permissible, is now a major deterrent to success. Effective writing also gains in importance, as email and text messaging becomes the most frequently used methods of business communication.

Time management is more than a tidy desk, an organized file system and efficient work habits. It is a continuing process that integrates technology with managerial and interpersonal skills directed toward a pre-determined goal in a way that maximizes the return on invested time. Technology is simply one ingredient in this effectiveness mix. It should be understood, used and controlled. But it should never be allowed to replace common sense, logic and sound management practice.

Manage Your Email

Leslie Bendaly, author of *Winner Instinct* says that she has met people who sort through more than one hundred emails daily. A poll of 26 top executives, conducted by Spencer Stuart's Chicago office, revealed that 76 percent of them spent at least one hour each day reading and responding to e-mail, with 12 percent spending more than three hours per day. Email, in spite of its timesaving qualities, can become a timewaster itself if not managed properly.

Don't interrupt yourself by continually checking your email throughout the day. Have specific mail times such as first thing in the morning and again after lunch. Checking messages at the end of the day is probably not a good idea since there's no time to take action. And you'll catch the mail in the morning anyway. Never check email until you have time to deal with it. Dispense with messages one at a time. Delete, file, respond or forward them. If they represent long-term tasks, transfer the needed information to your planner and delete the messages.

When an incoming e-mail merits a thank you, say nothing else. Don't add unnecessary comments that might encourage another reply in return. There is too much email that simply serves to thank others for thanking them. "You're welcome" is usually unnecessary. Don't feel compelled to get in the last word.

Don't clutter your electronic files with non-essential correspondence. Delete most email and only file those that you have to reference in the future. Print as few as possible and don't keep both printed and electronic versions. According to a survey conducted by Dianna Booher, of all the documents that are printed, copied and distributed by North American business every day, 75 to 80 percent are never referred to again. E-mail loses much of its advantage if it is printed. Yet, according to an article in the *Stouffville Tribune* (*Just Delete the Frustrations of E-Mail*, by Arthur Black,) 60 percent of all e-mail is still copied onto paper. Resist the urge to print your e-mail. Answer it, file it, or delete it. But don't keep it unless absolutely necessary.

When sending email, respect other people's time as well. Before you send that message to your entire mailing list, ask yourself a question. Would you send that many copies if it were paperwork? Send it only to those who need it or can benefit from it. Don't let the circulation list be determined by the ease of transmission.

Use a relevant header to make it easy to file. If you're replying to a message and changing the topic, take a few seconds to change the header to correspond with the new topic. Make sure the header grabs the reader's attention and immediately identifies the topic. The only way some people can cope with the overload of emails is to delete most unsolicited messages unread. They make this decision based on the header. A vague title such as "Opportunity" or "Thought you might be interested" could easily be deleted accidentally. If the receiver knows you, you might want to include your name in the header. And if you're replying to *their* e-mail, say so.

Although e-mail is sometimes viewed as a casual, conversational form of communication, it is rapidly becoming the accepted form of business communication as well. As such it warrants similar guidelines to that of hardcopy correspondence. Keep your message brief and indicate any action you want the reader to take. Limit each message to one topic. Use the Spell Checker feature; careless typing and sloppy grammar will reflect on both you *and* your company. Assume that all your email will be saved and viewed by others. Formality is even more important when corresponding to people in other countries who may not be accustomed to the more casual approach to communication.

There are dozens of symbols called emoticons representing the various emotions such as happiness, sadness etc., and even more abbreviations that people seem to be using, but I don't recommend either. Everyone is not familiar with them. Personally, we get annoyed when we encounter such hieroglyphics as LOL, IMHO or OTOH. It may save the writer a few seconds, but we waste our time trying to figure out what the gobbledygook means. We survived quite nicely without smiles, frowns and laughter symbols plastered in our written letters. Why the necessity now?

Walter H. Block and Jeff Senne, in their book, *CyberPower for Business* point out that computer screens are shorter than sheets of paper, so the most important information should be in the header and first paragraph or two of the message, where it is in full view. They say you can figure on about twenty lines of message.

A signature file, which could include your name, business name, telephone number, website address and one-line description of your business can be added automatically with most e-mail programs. It's unobtrusive at the end of the message, and in addition to its promotion value, helpful to the reader. And it compensates for the lack of a letterhead.

E-mail is one of the greatest timesaving marvels of the century. But like most things, if misused it can be as much a hindrance as help. Use it, but don't abuse it.

Don't buy into the technology myth

Using technology is essential. But by using technology indiscriminately, we are putting our lives into high gear, multitasking and filling our lives with incessant interruptions and trivia.

No generation has had as long a lifespan, yet a third of us claim we do not have enough time. In some respects, all we have done by introducing technology is to increase speed and reduce the time we spend on trivial, low-priority activities so we can take on more trivial low-priority activities.

For example, washing machines do a wash faster than grandmother`s scrubbing board; but now we have more clothes to wash and we wash them more often. Email is faster than writing or typing letters; but we send & receive more messages. We are driving faster; but have longer distances to travel, more traffic, more construction and more gridlock.

Life is being lived at a much faster pace than 50 years ago – or even 20 years ago. We have a love affair with speed. And it borders on the ridiculous. Fast-food restaurants carve 15 seconds off wait time, churches reduce the length of worship services, and publishers offer one-minute bedtime stories – children's stories reduced in length so we don't have to spend too much time with our toddlers at bedtime.

In spite of technology – or because of it - we are sacrificing sleep. The average person now gets 90 minutes less sleep a night then she did a century ago. Drowsiness causes more car accidents than alcohol. Getting less than 6 hours of sleep a night can impair motor coordination, speech, reflexes, productivity and judgment. We don't take time to eat properly, exercise properly or sleep sufficiently; about 20% of us are obese.

If we are walking faster, talking faster, driving faster, working faster, sleeping less, and using technology, why isn't productivity going through the roof, and what happened to all that extra leisure time that we were promised?

If you really want to manage your time, simplify your life. Time management is not doing more things in less time, which technology encourages, it is doing *fewer* things – things of *greater importance* - in the time that we have. Eliminate those possessions, activities, and To Do items that have little meaning to you or to the significant people in your life. That includes all those electronic gadgets that attract you and distract you. Be selective in the gadgets you use, and get rid of the ones that contribute nothing to your business or life purpose.

EPILOGUE

Putting the ideas into practice

The various ideas on saving time fall into two major categories: "mechanical ideas" and "behavioral ideas". The mechanical ideas are those that can be put into practice immediately without the necessity of a behavioral change. In other words, you don't have to form a new habit in order to make them work for you. An example would be changing the location of your telephone from your desk to the credenza behind you. When the phone rings you have to turn around to pick it up, which means you'll be facing the wall, with your back to the doorway. Since you will avoid eye contact, most people won't try to talk to you while you're on the phone. This idea will work immediately, since you don't have to form the habit of turning around - you have to turn around in order to pick up the phone.

Behavioral ideas are those that require effort on your part in order to make them work. You actually have to form a new habit, changing your behavior in the process. This could take weeks of persistence. For example, if you are currently in the habit of talking on the phone without making notes, a behavioral idea that could save time would be to start recording all calls in a systematic way. This ensures that nothing is forgotten, reduces follow-up calls, and increases concentration and so on. But you have to form the new habit before you can reap the rewards of the idea.

Mechanical ideas are plentiful, and since they require no behavior change, any number of them could be put into practice simultaneously. Although the time saved by each idea may be minimal, collectively they add up to hours. Behavioral ideas, on the other hand, would be overwhelming if you introduced more than one or two at a time. They take several weeks before they become habitual. But the payback, in terms of time saved, is usually much greater than the same number of mechanical ideas.

To form a new habit you must first become aware of your current behavior and then persistently act out the new behavior that you want to acquire - until it becomes the new behavior. To give you an idea of time involved, psychologists claim it takes 21 days to form a habit. Because the forming of habits is a gradual process, getting organized is a long-term process that could take months or even years.

Since small successes are motivational I suggest you start with a series of mechanical ideas. Clean up your work area, get rid of superfluous material, move your in-basket off your desk, make up a follow-up file, arrange your materials so they're close at hand. Then choose a behavioral idea that would eliminate a timewaster that you're experiencing. For example, if papers tend to accumulate on your desk and you waste time shuffling papers, build the habit of scheduling paperwork in the follow-up file for later action. If you are forever interrupting yourself and others as questions pop into your mind, start using a "Delegation Record" or "Communications Record" to accumulate those questions. If you're putting off important tasks because you don't have time, break the tasks into smaller chunks and schedule them in your planner to work on at specific times.

Each time a behavioral idea has been fully mastered, pick another one and work on it until it, too, has been incorporated into your daily routine.

Most behavioral ideas have a mechanical component as well. For example, making up a follow-up file is mechanical; but using it consistently the way it should be used is behavioral. Similarly, purchasing or making up your own *Personal Organizer* is mechanical, but consistently recording telephone calls in it is behavioral.

Mechanical ideas may have behavioral components as well, but minor ones or they would be classified as behavioral ideas. For example, although using a portable 3- hole punch, hand photocopier or pocket recorder is behavioral, it's hardly a deterrent when you need to punch a document, or copy a paragraph from something you don't want to forget. By comparison, try not to worry or not to procrastinate simply because you need to stop doing these things!

Not recognizing that there are two types of ideas could cause frustration on the part of individuals attempting to put them into practice. Many people give up after a few days either blaming the ideas or themselves, if they fail to work. But, in fact, the ideas that don't work are usually the "behavioral" ones that will take time to incorporate into their workday.

Don't be discouraged if you fail in your first attempts to put behavioral ideas into practice. And don't lay a guilt trip on yourself. Persistence pays off. You cannot get organized overnight. Work at it gradually. If something simply won't work, regardless of how hard you try, so be it. There are plenty of other ideas that will work. Remember you are a unique individual with unique personality, management style and thought process. Every idea that works for other people will not necessarily work for you.

Getting organized is a rewarding experience. It makes time for the important things in life. Remember, time management is not getting more done in less time; it is getting fewer things of great importance done in less time, with less stress, so life will become more meaningful and more enjoyable.

Have a great life!

APPENDIX

A time management checklist

Here are 50 time-tested ways of improving your personal productivity discussed in this or our other books and articles. Check those ideas that make sense to you, and yet are not currently being practiced on a regular basis.

___ 1. Put your business and sales goals and personal goals and policies in writing.

___ 2. Each week do something that brings you closer to your annual goals.

___ 3. Schedule *appointments with yourself* to complete priority work.

___ 4. Schedule more time for tasks and appointments than you think they will take.

___ 5. Set priorities according to importance, not urgency.

___ 6. Make notes while you are talking on the telephone or meeting with a customer.

___ 7. Never rely on your memory; write things down.

___ 8. Develop the *do it now* habit. Don't procrastinate.

___ 9. Don't confuse activity with results. Time management is not doing *more* things, but *more important* things.

___ 10. Take advantage of travel time and commute time to plan, create and relax.

___ 11. Delete as many emails as possible once they are completed.

___ 12. Don't write an email message when a telephone call will do.

___ 13. Make minor decisions quickly.

___ 14. Set deadlines on all tasks that you schedule or delegate.

___ 15. Be time conscious rather than a perfectionist. Let work time proportionate to the value of the outcome.

___ 16. Arrive on time for all appointments. If you arrive early, use the time for important administrative tasks.

___ 17. Keep telephone conversations brief; discuss the business up front.

___ 18. Write brief letters, reports and e-mail. Encourage brevity in others.

___ 19. When a crisis occurs, immediately determine how to stop a recurrence.

___ 20. Say "no" more often. Have as much respect for your own time as you have for other people's time.

___ 21. Don't keep shuffling papers; handle each item only once whenever possible. Do it, scrap it, file it, delegate it or schedule a time to do it later. Use a similar procedure for electronic mail.

___ 22. Use a follow-up file to hold paperwork relating to scheduled tasks.

___ 23. Manage your sales territory to minimize lost time, wait time and travel time.

___ 24. Take advantage of timesaving technology such as voice activated software and text replacement   software.

___ 25. Have an objective for every sales call or meeting.

___ 26. Start earlier in the morning. Utilize your *prime time* for priorities.

___ 27. Don't keep magazines. Tear out or photocopy relevant articles and keep them in a "Read" file.

___ 28. Spend less time on the lower-priority administrative tasks and more time on revenue-producing activities.

___ 29. Record the whole year's schedule of meetings, events etc. into your planner as they become known.

___ 30. Always carry a small scratch pad, pocket recorder or PDA to record notes and capture ideas.

___ 31. Use the same planner for home and office. Schedule time for family events as well as work.

___ 32. Be in control of your own life; don't let others' lack of planning become your crisis.

___ 33. Have set times each day to review your e-mail. Assign time limits.

___ 34. Always take a few minutes after each sales call or meeting to evaluate how it went.

___ 35. If someone calls for an appointment, try to settle the matter right then on the telephone.

___ 36. When leaving a message for someone, indicate a convenient time to call back.

___ 37. If the person you're calling is not in, try to get the information you need from someone else.

___ 38. Record the time you must leave the office when traveling to a distant meeting or appointment.

___ 39. If items dropped in your in-basket distract you, move the basket from your desk.

___ 40. When away on a business trip, have someone else sort and dispense with most of your mail.

___ 41. Heed the 80/20 Rule. Spend more time with the high-potential customers.

___ 42. When filing paperwork, record a *throw out* date on it to make subsequent purging easier.

___ 43. Always confirm appointments before leaving the home or office.

___ 44. Hold brief breakfast meetings when most people are mentally alert and have a full day to take action.

___ 45. Capture ideas when listening to audio recordings by dictating into a pocket recorder or smart phone.

___ 46. Use checklists for recurring events such as meetings and business trips.

___ 47. Spend time each week on *time investments* – those activities that will help you free up more time, such as training, self-development, creativity sessions and adequate sleep and exercise.

___ 48. When putting something in your follow-up file, make a corresponding note in your planner to say it's there.

___ 49. Every evening, review your plans for the next day and make adjustments when appropriate.

___ 50. Manage stress by putting life in perspective, and not taking yourself too seriously. Recognize that you can't do everything. Focus on priorities and keep a positive attitude.

Other suggestions:

___

___

___

___ Total ideas checked

CONCLUDING WORDS

Action Sheet

In order to get started, choose three ideas that make sense to you, and that you would be willing to start practicing. Record them in the spaces below, select a starting date, and go to it! Remember to persist for 4 weeks to allow time for a habit to develop in the event that the ideas are *behavioral* in nature. Once they are working successfully, choose three more and work on those.

1. _____

2. _____

3. _____

How to implement the ideas

The ideas listed on the time management checklist are either *mechanical ideas* or *behavioral ideas*. Mechanical ideas are those that can be put into practice immediately without the necessity of a behavioral change. In other words, you don't have to form a new habit in order to make them work for you. For example, changing the location of your telephone from your desk to the credenza behind you is a mechanical idea. When the phone rings you have to turn around to pick it up, which means you'll be facing the wall, with your back to the doorway. Since you will avoid eye contact, most people won't try to talk to you while you're on the phone. This idea will work immediately, since you don't have to form the habit of turning around — you *have* to turn around in order to pick up the phone.

Behavioral ideas are those that require a behavioral change in order to make them work. You have to form a new habit. This could take weeks of persistence. For example, if you are currently in the habit of talking on the phone without making notes, a behavioral idea that could save time would be to start recording all calls in a systematic way. This ensures that nothing is forgotten, reduces follow-up calls, increases concentration and so on. But you have to form the new habit before you can reap the rewards of the idea. Mechanical ideas are plentiful, and since they require no behavior change, any number of them could be put into practice simultaneously. Although the time saved by each idea may be minimal, collectively they add up to hours. Behavioral ideas, on the other hand, would be overwhelming if you introduced more than one or two at a time. They take several weeks before they become habitual. But the payback, in terms of time saved, is usually much greater than the same number of mechanical ideas.

Since small successes are motivational I suggest you start with a series of mechanical ideas. Clean up your work area, get rid of superfluous material, move your in basket off your desk, make up a follow-up file, arrange your materials so they're close at hand. Then choose a behavioral idea that would eliminate a time waster that you're experiencing. For example, if papers tend to accumulate on your desk and you waste time shuffling papers, build the habit of scheduling paperwork in the follow-up file for later action. If you are forever interrupting yourself and others as questions pop into your mind, start using a *Delegation Record* or *Communications Record to* accumulate those questions. If you're putting off important tasks because you don't have time, break the tasks into smaller chunks and schedule them in your planner to work on at specific times. Each time a behavioral idea has been fully mastered, pick another one and work on it until it, too, has been incorporated into your daily routine.

Making time work for you

Once you are successful in implementing a dozen or more of the ideas introduced at this time management session, you will have freed up some time. Use this time to work on some of the time investments explained earlier. For example, train someone else to take over one of your tasks, learn a new timesaving software program or spend an hour every Friday afternoon planning the next week. Continually re-investing the additional time that you have freed up will result in increased effectiveness in turn. This process is referred to as making time work for you.

Implement a new idea each week
It's important to continue to implement timesaving techniques in the weeks and years ahead. You can subscribe to a free monthly electronic newsletter that offers quick tips in addition to a brief article. If you apply only one idea each week, your personal productivity will increase immensely during the course of a year. You can subscribe to this newsletter at www.taylorintime.com. Other free resources are available at the website as well.

RECOMMENDED RESOURCES

Free eBooks

You can download free eBooks in PDF format at Bookboon.com.

Two of our books published by Bookboon that contain additional ideas, including how to work effectively in the digital age of speed, are:

Time to be productive: how to develop your time management skills

Time Management Strategies for an ADHD World

Other Books

Found at www.coachingyourdownline.com: *Coaching Your Downline to Become Your Successline*

Found at www.TaylorinTime.com: *Taylor Time Planner (day planner)* and several other books

Wealth of Online Resources

FREE Taylor Monthly Newsletter – register at www.TaylorinTime.com

Coaching Programs for Network Marketers - described at www.CoachingYourDownline.com

"Making Time Work For You" Podcasts - www.Youtube.com/user/MakingTimeWorkforYou

Holistic time management - www.mindsontime.com

Speaking Engagements, Coaching and Training Services

Contact us for details
Tel: (905)970-0955   Email: phoenixdistribution@bell.net

Endorsements

As a network marketer who wants your time to be both productive and profitable, you need 'Time Management for Network Marketers' in your success library. Actually, I'd suggest you have a well-thumbed, re-read version close at hand to remind you of the importance of each minute you strategically invest in building your business. Recruiting, training and equipping, hand-holding (at times), SELLING, leading and keeping your team focused and productive requires a great deal of your time, discipline, and energy. Remaining focused and keeping your own energies high does too! As a leading network marketer, 'YOU' need to be better organized and disciplined in leveraging your time if you want to profitably succeed and help your team members. My friends Harold Taylor and Garry Ford have carefully created this time enhancing resource to help you and your teams profitably grow and succeed. I have been a long-time client and fan of Harold Taylor and still use his Taylor Planner as a part of my own success strategies. These timely success tips and strategies really work and have helped me productively leverage my time for some amazing successes over the years.
~ Bob 'Idea Man' Hooey, Egremont Alberta - Accredited Speaker, author of the best-selling Legacy of Leadership, 2011 Spirit of CAPS recipient (Canadian Association of Professional Speakers)

I am sorry that I have known Garry for only a few years. I live and work in the UK, so during that time we have usually been separated by at least five time zones 4,000 miles and nearly 8 hours of flight time, often in online meetings chaired by Garry in Canada, with fellow directors on both sides of Australia. Our time management has always been critical to the success of our collaboration, and it soon became clear to me that Garry is a rare master of the art and science of time management. Before I met Garry my idea of time management went no further than the useful "Do, Designate, Delegate or Ditch" mantra. As time passes, "Goals can keep you young" becomes even more valuable. Here is a man who not only talks the talk but also walks the walk. There is no better person to equip network marketers with this all-important tool. The book contains excellent lessons for all, network marketers or not, and the time invested in reading this book and building its lessons into your daily life is time very well spent.
~ Nick Mallett, London England – Attorney and Director of Nick Mallett Consulting

I'm extremely pleased that someone finally took the time to address one of the most important aspects of building a successful Network Marketing business - time management. Regardless of the company, product, or compensation plan, if you don't make the effort to develop good time management skills, your ability to reach the highest echelons and become one of the top income earners within the NWM industry will be greatly compromised. Having worked with Carol Ford, I can certainly attest to the fact that she is highly proficient, extraordinarily professional, and very knowledgeable about every aspect of the industry. The golden nuggets she and her husband share in this book are priceless.
~ Marcus A. Okopny, Markham Ontario and Florida - 20 year NWM veteran

I've had the pleasure of working with both Garry and Carol Ford for over 12 years. I've witnessed how they can take a small business and turn it into an empire in a very short period of time. They are some of the most innovative and devoted people in their field.
~ Robert Tomilson, Oakville Ontario - DNM, R.BIE, R.Ac.

Time Management seems to be the most crucial pitfall of network marketers and this book has great insights and practical step by step chapters in truly understanding the value of time and managing time effectively. Every network marketer who wants to achieve exciting new goals should study this book and take the action steps outlined for success!
~ Colleen Walters, Ohio - CEO and Founder (of global direct selling company)

I've known Garry and Carol for a long time, having worked in the network marketing industry both in the field and at the corporate level. Garry also served for several years on the Board of Directors of the Direct Sellers Association (DSA). Garry and Carol have coached many network marketing entrepreneurs and leaders to achieve the success that only comes from persistence in goal setting, effective use of time, and putting first things first. They have seen how great potential can be squandered by a lack of time management and focused effort. Who better than Garry and Carol Ford, industry icons, and Harold Taylor, the guru of time management, to take you step by step to success as a network marketing entrepreneur! I urge you to not only read this book, but to put its principles into everyday practice!
~ Peter Gothe, North Carolina - President, Alliance Business Concepts Inc.

I have known Garry and Carol Ford for over 25 years - and in fact, Garry Ford is the single most person who has taught me, shown me, coached me and mentored me back in my very early and very green days in this industry. Where I am today, I owe to Garry Ford. The wisdom of his mind, the gentleness of his heart and the lifelong commitment he has made to this industry is something to be cherished. I recommend not just reading whatever is written, but to truly embrace it!
~ Sheila Hercules, Toronto Ontario - Senior Management with direct selling company

Throughout my 19-year career in network marketing (direct sales), I have seen a consistent theme of distributors not managing their time effectively. Mostly, it has led them to quit the business and talk negatively about the industry. Thank you for producing this book as I know it will resolve one of the reasons distributors fail in our industry. I enjoyed reading it and I know others will as well.
~ Jim Lupkin, Social Media Trainer & Coach to the direct sales industry

What a wonderful book—and long overdue! I have been involved in network marketing for 40 years and have learnt to follow the principles outlined in this book. I have known Garry and Carol Ford for quite a few years and have worked with them in Canada and internationally. I cannot think of better or more qualified individuals to write this book—people who have actually done it, rather than just talk about it. They are true network marketers, and their accomplishments speak for themselves. This book gives a good framework to follow for what is required in order to be successful in network marketing. Many people come into this type of business and think they can succeed without understanding the various steps needed to be successful. This book spells it all out. By following the principles outlined, you can become a true leader—not a follower. I highly recommend this book.
~ Brian B Jacques, Florida and UK - International Entrepreneur and Professional Network Marketer

Carol Ford has demonstrated over time the critical need for companies to be organized, focused and absolutely diligent in the way they partner with their independent distributors. As field leaders match this corporate commitment and treat their business seriously in the way they manage their time and efforts, success becomes the natural result. When working together, virtually nothing is impossible."
~ Rick S. Nelson, Utah - Direct selling international development expert. Highly skilled professional in laying foundations and building markets that support hundreds of millions of dollars in sales around the world.

Time Management for Network Marketers is sure to be a prized desk top reference book to make a difference to all network marketers, as well as for anyone wanting to master their time and manage their life to make it fulfilling and productive. Make sure to take lots of notes and perhaps highlight the important parts of this book for quick reference.
~ Megs and Ramila Padiachy, Ottawa Ontario - Health Practitioners and Master Gold Managers

What may take time but will gain you much time and greater success? If you want to prevent hours of wasted time building your business, if you need to identify things you may be doing that don't relate to your goals, if you need to manage yourself better and if you want practical, do-able steps to get better organized….this book contains hundreds of practical, do-able proven ideas that can be implemented immediately. The tips and techniques will benefit not only your business but also your personal life. If you are naturally organized, you will find tips and techniques to enhance your productivity. If you were born disorganized, there is hope for you in this book!
~ Ruth Wong, Hawaii - ORGANIZATION PLUS

Entrepreneurship is on the rise, but there are only a few people that will be really successful. The dividing line between a successful entrepreneur and a struggling one is the knowledge that is found in this book created for your success. Garry and Carol have done a wonderful job accumulating all you will ever need to know to attain the success that you deserve.
~ Wally Kralik, Lakefield Ontario - Professional networker who has earned millions of dollars by helping create millionaires in his wellness company.

As the authors remind us, it takes money, people and time to run a successful business. Only one can't be replaced. I've been following and benefiting from Harold's wisdom since the early 80's. Following his insights and philosophy has enabled me to find the time to read a book a week (over a three-year period), and write three books which resulted in getting calls to work with the largest companies in Canada. If you are interested in taking control of your time, earning more money and getting more out of your life... buy and apply this book. You might not be able to replace your time, but this book provides a map to clearly and easily find more time to do what you want!
~ Tom Stoyan, Kleinburg Ontario - Canada Sales Coach

As an entrepreneur, my business interests are not only diverse but time consuming – Interestingly two of them are themed along the lines of "TIME". I have found that time management is the greatest tool entrepreneurs are in need of, but lack the knowledge of how to "take the time" to 'watch' their time. This book promises an insightful (and might I say) "timely' publication that will no doubt stand the 'test of time' and serve us all well. I fully believe in the authors' ability to offer strategic and practical planning information through this new exciting book that will serve anyone in any industry well.
~ P.C.Harris, Mississauga Ontario - CCO PCHARRIS COMMUNICATIONS

Time Management is a life-lesson that has to be learned. Gary Ford continues to provide common-sense advice on how to become successful through creating the right habits. He clearly shows the steps and the thought process to manage your time more effectively...which results in managing your life. This book is a must read for everyone, no matter your vocation or income level. A concise road map based on the authors' successful careers and personal lives.
~ Rob Hukezalie, USA – President, RMH Consulting

I have watched Carol Ford for 10+ years as both a network marketing professional and as a direct sales company executive. She is extremely talented as a speaker who can excite a crowd with her upbeat positive attitude and humor, but can get down in the trenches with a person just journeying this exciting industry which needs some coaching and advice. I recommend her coaching to anyone who wants to accelerate their business growth.
~ Carl Stanitzky, CSA, CLTC, MBA – Senior Ranks for 40 Years in Network Marketing industry

Covering everything from planning to procrastination, Time Management for Network Marketers is
an easy-to-read, quick-to-digest handbook full of critical time management tactics. Implement them
and you'll be forever confident you're using your most precious resource effectively. From one of the most respected time management gurus, Harold Taylor, comes a book dedicated to motivating network marketers to make the most of their time. Like any entrepreneur in charge of creating their own schedule and mastering self-discipline, it can be easy to squander and misuse time. Investing time to read and implement the practical ideas in this book will pay itself back many times over. Use it to unlock your personal and professional success.
~Clare Kumar, Professional Organizer and Productivity Consultant, Streamlife Ltd.

Printed in Great Britain
by Amazon.co.uk, Ltd.,
Marston Gate.